BLACK PANTHERS
FOR BEGINNERS®

HERB BOYD

ILLUSTRATIONS BY
LANCE TOOKS

FOR BEGINNERS®

For Beginners LLC
155 Main Street, Suite 211
Danbury, CT 06810 USA
www.forbeginnersbooks.com

A For Beginners® Documentary Comic Book
Copyright © 2015

Cataloging-in-Publication information is available from the Library of Congress.

ISBN # 978-1-939994-39-4 Trade

Manufactured in the United States of America

For Beginners® and Beginners Documentary Comic Books® are published by For
Beginners LLC.

First Edition

10 9 8 7 6 5 4 3 2 1

CONTENTS

To the fallen Panthers who dared to challenge one of the world's most oppressive governments, and especially to Mike Tabor, Connie Matthews, Dhoruba and Tanaquil, and Mumia Abu-Jamal.

-- H.B.

My thanks to Writers and Readers for the opportunity to help create this book, to the Black Panthers for giving so much to try and make things better, and to my family for everything else.

-- L.T.

A crowd of onlookers gawked from the sidewalk as four young black men dressed in black leather jackets and berets leaped from a Volkswagen, each of them wielding pump shotguns with bandoliers strapped across their bodies. The young men surrounded two white police officers who had accosted a black man and had him spread-eagled against a building.

The young men did not say a word as the police officers watched them nervously, their eyes fixed on the shotguns.

One of the young men held a large law book in his hand, waiting to recite their Constitutional rights to bear arms and to observe the police's actions.

Under the fierce gaze of the young black men the police stopped their arrest procedures, returned to their patrol car and drove off.

This was the Black Panther Party in ideal action. The real story—the whole story—was both more and less heroic.

In the fall of 1966, **Huey Newton** and **Bobby Seale**, both students at Merritt Junior College in Oakland, California, decided that they had lost all faith in the government of America.

They were sick of the Federal Government's brutal policy of "benign neglect," furious with local politicians more interested in stuffing their own pockets than in helping the poor and hungry, and they were sick to death of the civil rights movement and its out-of-touch old leaders who still counseled moderation and nonviolence after all those years of useless promises. To hell with moderation and nonviolence! It was time to stop singing and to start swinging! It was time to stop talking and to start fighting back.

For the next several minutes the two friends hashed out the platform for the Black Panther Party, exchanging ideas, with Newton reciting and Seale taking notes.

In less than an hour they had outlined the **Ten Point Program**.

1

We want freedom. We want power to determine the destiny of our community. We believe that Black people will not be free until we are able to determine our destiny.

4

Marcus Garvey

Whether they knew it or not, Newton and Seale's list of demands and beliefs were nearly identical to earlier ten point programs proposed by Marcus Garvey and Elijah Muhammad. Their next task was to decide who did what.

"What do you want to be, Bobby? Chairman or Minister of Defense?"

"It makes me no difference."

"Okay, I'll be the Minister of Defense and you'll be the Chairman..."

"That's fine with me."

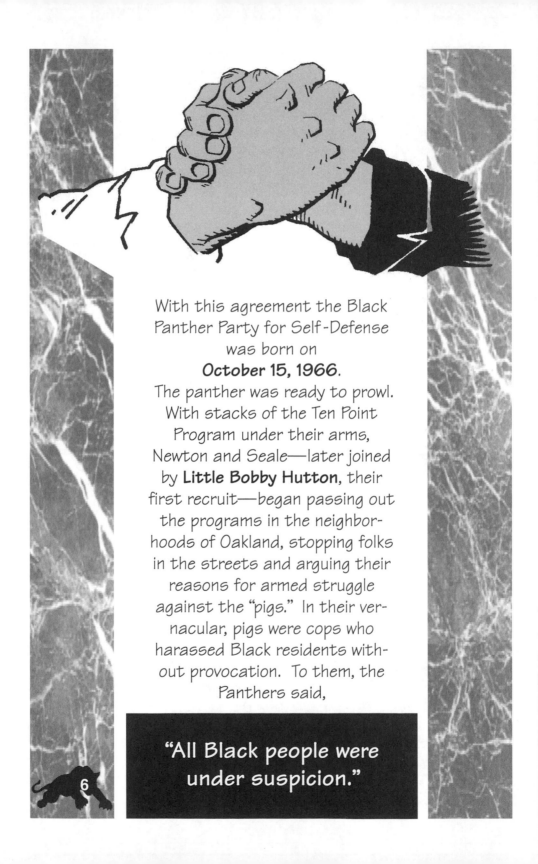

With this agreement the Black
Panther Party for Self-Defense
was born on
October 15, 1966.
The panther was ready to prowl.
With stacks of the Ten Point
Program under their arms,
Newton and Seale—later joined
by **Little Bobby Hutton,** their
first recruit—began passing out
the programs in the neighbor-
hoods of Oakland, stopping folks
in the streets and arguing their
reasons for armed struggle
against the "pigs." In their ver-
nacular, pigs were cops who
harassed Black residents without provocation. To them, the
Panthers said,

**"All Black people were
under suspicion."**

People the trio of Panthers encountered on the streets were stunned by the new group's boldness and wondered why they had chosen a panther as their symbol.

Newton, who was never at a loss for an answer, explained: **"The nature of the panther is that he never attacks. But if anyone attacks him or backs him into a corner the panther comes up to wipe the aggressor or that attacker out."**

Newton and Seale decided that these Panthers needed guns.

Actually, there was nothing new about using the panther as a symbol, or about Black people using guns. Several months before Newton and Seale started the Panthers, the Lowndes County Freedom Party of Alabama had declared the panther the symbol of their party.

A few years before Newton and Seale conceived their plans, militant activist Robert Williams expressed his outrage against racism in his book *Negroes with Guns*:

"All those who dare to attack are going to learn the hard way that the Afro-American is not a pacifist; that he cannot forever be counted on not to defend himself. Those who attack him brutally and ruthlessly can no longer expect to attack him with impunity."

8

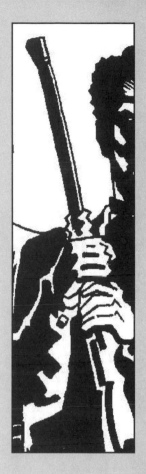

Newton and Seale were no fools: They not only carried guns, they studied law books. From the law books they read, Newton and Seale learned that it was permissible to carry an unconcealed, unloaded rifle or a shotgun in California. Because Newton was on probation, he couldn't carry a pistol; so, Seale carried the pistol, and Newton shouldered an unloaded M-1 rifle. When they were accosted by the police, they would recite the Second Amendment of the Constitution about the people's right to bear arms:

"A well-regulated militia, being necessary to the security of a free state, the right of the people to keep and bear arms shall not be infringed."

Residents of the Black community would see the Panthers coming and run for cover. The question on everybody's mind—which nobody had the nerve to ask—was: "Who in the world are those crazy radicals?"

"Power flows from the barrel of a gun,"

"Power flows from the barrel of a gun..."

was one of Mao Tse-Tung's famous quotes, and it was while selling Mao's Little Red Book to earn money to buy the guns that the young Panthers adopted both the spirit and letter of Mao's words and became, in their own eyes, revolutionaries..

9

The Panthers admired the militant philosophy of **Malcolm X** -- especially his advocacy of armed self-defense.

"WE'RE GOING TO BE THE PERSONIFICATION OF MALCOLM'S DREAMS," Newton told his comrades.

Malcolm called for freedom and justice "BY ANY MEANS NECESSARY!"

The Panthers, at rallies and marches, screamed in unison, "POWER TO THE PEOPLE!"

It all came down to the same thing, didn't it?

10

2

We want full employment for our people.

11

Inspired by Malcolm's legacy and funded by the sales of Mao's Red Book, the Panthers expanded their activist agenda and stepped up their plan to defend the community.

"We'll protect a mother, protect a brother, and protect the community from racist cops..."

...Seale proclaimed in his autobiography *Seize the Time*.

"And in turn we get brothers in the organization and they will in turn relate to the Red Book. They will relate to political, economic, and social equality in defense of the community."

The activity that really put the Panthers on the map was "policing the police."

There were only 19 Blacks out of 600 officers on the Oakland police force, so the Panthers, to say the least, had their hands full. They were so **balsy** that they actually followed the Oakland police around. Whenever they encountered the police harassing or arresting somebody, Newton, Seale, and Li'l Bobby Hutton would jump from their car and approach the officers.

Brandishing a camera, a tape recorder, a law book, and with their guns in full view, they would stand off to the side and make sure the police conducted themselves within the law. **"So long as we remain the proper distance from you,"** Newton often told the police, **"we can observe what you do. This is not interfering or disorderly conduct."**

Their policing the police was quickly the talk of the town. It was also the talk of every law enforcement agency in the country. It was only a matter of time before the Panthers aggressive monitoring provoked a showdown with the nervous, racist police officers... .

AND EVERYBODY ON BOTH SIDES KNEW IT.

13

The Panthers didn't invent the idea of keeping tabs on cops. A similar plan was started in Los Angeles after the Watts riots in 1965. But the Panthers took the idea a step—a GIANT STEP— further: They used guns! They did it in a perfectly legal way— and their patrols were successful. Too successful: The police stopped harassing the citizens and turned their attention on the Panthers themselves.

Not long after the Panthers opened their first office in Oakland on January 1, 1967, the police accosted Newton and Seale in a car with other Panthers parked in front of their office. With his cohorts as the audience, Newton put on a daring, if reckless performance. It was a proverbial Mexican standoff, and Newton never blinked.

"What are you doing with that gun?" an officer asked Newton, after following him from his car into Panther headquarters.

"What are you doing with your gun?" Newton snapped back. **"Because if you try to shoot at me, or if you try to take this gun, I'm going to shoot back at you, swine."**

Unnerved by Huey's defiance, the officer muttered something under his breath and then stammered:

"You're just trying to turn the Constitution around."

Earlier in the encounter, Newton had refused to answer the officer's questions, citing the Fifth Amendment and the right of individuals not to incriminate themselves.

"I'm not turning anything around," Huey responded.

Another officer, equally upset by Newton's antics, began badgering the Panther leader. "Are you a Marxist?" the husky officer asked.

"Are you a fascist?" Huey replied.

For several minutes the two went back and forth, the remarks becoming louder and more intense. This bit of bravado by Newton delighted his friends and admirers, who were amused by the remarks and how they infuriated the police.

Soon the word reverberated throughout the community. "The Panthers don't take no shit; not even from the police." "Either Newton and the Panthers are the bravest or the craziest people in the world." Young neighborhood Blacks were excited by the Panthers' courage, and the more adventurous of them were among the Party's first recruits.

In asserting their rights as citizens the Panthers were actually acting in the proudest tradition of America.

15

Their acts were consistent with the rugged individualism and the desire for freedom and dignity that had characterized the behavior of the so-called Founding Fathers of this nation. If there was anything unAmerican about the Panthers' story, it was the repressive and brutal behavior of the Police. From the beginning, the Panthers could see that there was no trick, no deception the police would not use to stifle the rise of the Black Panther Party.

But they had work to do, and it couldn't wait.

16

3

We want an end to robbery by the Capitalists of our Black community.

The Panthers drew their early recruits from the Black working class and the poverty stricken districts of East Oakland. Many of them were high school dropouts, ex-felons, drug users and peddlers, petty hustlers and gang bangers. They were a gaggle of "basic bloods from off the block" ready to throw down, and who sometimes sang:

"There's a pig on the hill/If you don't get 'im, the Panthers will."

18

Even if they had been employable, there were few jobs available in a city where the unemployment rate was almost twice the national average. Complementing this ragtag crew were a number of Panthers who attended college, held down full-time jobs, or were merely impressionable youth eager for any kind of action.

Attraction to the Panthers was not limited, however, to just teenagers; a gaggle of older men and women, Black and white, fell under the spell of the Panther mystique. Eldridge Cleaver recalled his first meeting with the Panthers:

"I fell in love with the Black Panther Party immediately upon my first encounter with it; it was literally love at first sight," Cleaver gushed. "It happened one night at a meeting in a dingy little storefront on Scott Street in the Fillmore District, the heart of San Francisco's Black ghetto. It was February 1967....I spun around in my seat and saw the most beautiful sight I had ever seen; four Black men wearing black berets, powder blue shirts, black leather jackets, black trousers, shiny black shoes—and each with a gun!"

19

That a hardened felon, an ex-rapist, who had spent a good part of his youth in prison, could be struck with such awe epitomized the seductive power of the Panthers. A recent parolee from Soledad Prison where he had served nine years of a fourteen year sentence for rape, Cleaver, then 33, was working as a senior editor at *Ramparts* magazine and would soon gain national acclaim when his book **Soul on Ice** hit the bestseller list.

Cleaver was among a number of local activists at this meeting when he met the Panthers for the first time in full regalia. The meeting was called to discuss a commemoration of Malcolm X who had been slain two years earlier. Malcolm's widow, Betty Shabazz, was invited to give the keynote address at the Bayview Community Center in Hunter's Point, and the task of security was split between Newton and Seale's party and the Black Panther Party of Northern

California, a group declaring it was the original Panthers. (Groups from various parts of the country have claimed, at one time or another, to have been the original original Panthers, but there is no hard evidence to prove that claim. That doesn't mean they're wrong. The time is so right for some things that they seem to happen spontaneously in several places at the same time. But that quintessential Panther moment—confronting the police with law books and rifles, could only happen in states where it's legal to carry a gun in public.)

POWER TO THE PEOPLE

When Shabazz arrived for the memorial, she was escorted by the members of the two Panther groups and everything went off without a hitch until Newton discovered that the Panthers from Northern California were carrying unloaded weapons. Protecting Malcolm's widow with unloaded weapons—they may as well have been using water pistols! Newton was furious. He told the Northerners they had three choices: join Newton's Panthers, change their name, or disband. They found none of the options to their liking. Newton and his Panthers made it plain that they were not jiving. The group changed its name.

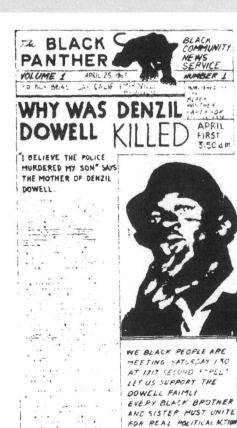

By the spring of 1967, the Panther party had increased its numbers, published its first mimeographed newsletter, and gained wider recognition for its brazen contempt for the police, who by now were always referred to as the "pigs."

As the newsletter improved in quality and circulation, the caricatures of the police, thanks to the illustrations of **Emory Douglas,** were hilariously rendered.

Each of them possessed a huge, fiendish snout, pointed ears, and a protruding corkscrew tail. It was the Panthers way of turning the tables on an enemy whom they felt viewed them as less than human.

The popularity of the Panthers spread rapidly, but they were still virtually unknown outside of California. One act was necessary to propel them into the national spotlight, and it occurred on May 2, 1967, in Sacramento at the State Capitol Building.

When the caravan of cars came to a halt outside the Capitol Building, thirty Black Panthers—twenty-four men and six women—emerged. All of them were dressed in black and some of them had bandoliers criss-crossing their bodies with rifles and shotguns pointed down to the ground or straight up in the air.

23

With a holstered 9mm pistol strapped to his waist, Bobby Seale led the way as the Panthers fanned out and walked toward the Capitol Building. Suddenly, from out of nowhere came a virtual army of reporters. Lights from the TV cameras and flashbulbs illuminated the band of young Panthers as they went from room to room, looking for the State Assembly meeting hall.

Onlookers were stunned at the procession, gawking and muttering to each other: "Who in the hell are these crazy Negroes?" The Panthers were unaware that one of the shocked, muttering, spectators was Governor Ronald Reagan.

24

Entering the Assembly floor, Seale was surprised that Cleaver was there and even more surprised when Cleaver joined the Panthers as they filed down the aisle. Having reached a strategic point, the Panthers stopped, and Seale unrolled the paper he had clutched in his hand and read the Party's **"Executive Mandate number One"**:

"The Black Panther Party for Self-Defense calls upon the American people in general and the Black people in particular to take careful note of the racist California Legislature which is now considering legislation aimed at keeping the Black people disarmed and powerless at the very same time that racist police agencies throughout the country are intensifying the terror, brutality, murder, and repression of Black people."

The media all across the nation picked up the story. It was not the words that kept eyes riveted to the reports; it was the image of Black men bearing arms. It was a dazzling show of force; but the Panther's gun display backfired on them. Instead of halting the push for gun-control laws then on the minds of many legislators, the invasion only sped up the introduction of new measures to check the possibility of another Panther embar-

25 cents

THE BLACK PANTHER
Black Community News Service

VOLUME 1   MAY 15, 1967   NUMBER 2

PUBLISHED WEEKLY BY **THE BLACK PANTHER PARTY FOR SELF DEFENSE**   P. O. Box 8641 Emeryville Brd Oakland, Calif.

The Truth About SACRAMENTO

TO BLOODS

TO COPS

Statement BY MINISTER OF DEFENSE TO THE BLACK WORLD

SUPPORT YOUR LOCAL POLICE

rassment. Having made their point in a most dramatic fashion thanks largely to the media, the Panthers wisely decided to develop a media network/ propaganda machine of their own. They started a newsletter and gradually expanded it to a bona fide newspaper, loaded with inflammatory rhetoric. Because he possessed considerable writing skills, Cleaver took over as editor of the paper. Then there was the matter of creating a Party icon, a symbol that would help bring in even more members.

That was an easy decision. Have the handsome Newton—dressed in his typical Panther garb with his beret at just the right angle—sit in a broad-backed rattan chair, a zebra-skin rug under his feet, bracket him with a couple of African shields, and place a spear in his right hand and a shot gun in his left and, voila! One of the most popular posters of the sixties.

27

Young people who had no idea who or what the Panthers were all about soon placed Newton posters on their walls alongside Elvis, John Coltrane, Malcolm X, Marilyn Monroe, Muhammad Ali, and Jimi Hendrix. In theory, Huey Newton opposed the "cult of personality" implications of his poster; in reality, it fed his considerable ego. Bottom line: It was a great poster that helped to put the Panthers on the political map.

But it was just the beginning. In the succeeding months the Panthers commanded the headlines and no Black face was as immediately recognizable as Newton's. His boyish features, macho gaze, and muscular body seemed straight from central casting. Newton was also, according to close associates, a mental case with a quick temper. And given the right circumstances and audience he was capable of the most bizarre, unruly behavior. In October, 1967, almost a year to the day of the founding of the Black Panther Party, Newton clashed violently with the law, and within a few hours after the incident not only would his face be well-known in America but...we're getting ahead of ourselves.

Much of what happened on that early morning is a matter of conjecture; what can be said for certain is that Newton was on his way home from a party celebrating the ending of his probation with a friend when Officer John Frey in his patrol car asked Newton to pull over. From the car's license plate, Officer Frey knew the car was registered to a member of the Panther party.

"Well, I'll be. If it isn't the great Huey Newton..."

...the officer said in a sing-song fashion.

"Let me see your driver's license and registration."

Frey took the documents, looked them over, passed Newton his license but kept the registration, which he took with him to his car. Obviously Frey had telephoned for help, for within minutes patrolman Herbert Heanes was on the scene. When Frey returned from checking the registration, he asked Newton and his companion, Gene McKinney, to get out of the car.

The officer asked Newton to walk over to his patrol car.

"**You have no reason to arrest me,**" Newton asserted, opening his law book to cite a passage.

30

"**You can take that law book and shove it up your ass,**" Officer Frey replied.

A scuffle broke out, gunfire erupted, and when the shooting was over, Newton had been shot in the stomach, Officer Heanes had multiple wounds, and Officer Frey was dead. Newton's companion, Gene McKinney, fled.

But a gentleman named Dell Ross told a different story:

Ross claimed that he happened to be driving by the scene when Newton and McKinney flagged him down and at gun point made him drive them to a nearby destination, then they both took off running. Newton made it to David Hilliard's house who in turn took him to Kaiser Hospital. At the hospital Newton was handled roughly by the police, handcuffed, and denied immediate medical attention. A news photographer at the scene snapped a picture of Huey Newton, only this time he wasn't posing for a poster. His naked torso, pierced by a policeman's bullet, turned up on the front page of every newspaper in America.

And if that wasn't bad enough, an impaneled grand jury returned a three-count indictment against Newton. The wounded Panther was charged with first-degree murder, assault with a deadly weapon, and the kidnapping of Dell Ross. Now the party and the Black movement had its cause celèbre and slowly the cries of "Free Huey" began to resound across the country. "In less than a week we're in action, borrowing a psyche-delically painted double-deck bus from one of the local white political communes, cruising the streets blaring 'Free Huey! Free Huey! Can a black man get a fair trial in America—even if he was defending his life against a white policeman?" David Hilliard recalled in his searing autobiography **This Side of Glory**. Hilliard, Newton's lifelong friend and the party's Chief of Staff, said that with this incident Newton became a national fig-ure, thanks largely to large rallies created by the Huey Newton Defense Committee.

HUEY MUST BE SET FREE

The first rallies and marches were held at the courthouse with brothers and sisters chanting: **"Free Huey, Free Huey, Free Huey, or the sky's the limit!"** Soon it was a kind of shared mantra that reverberated beyond the radical community, uniting folks around the world who were interested in social justice and political freedom.

"In February we host the grand birthday party [Newton was born February 17, 1942] attended by H. Rap Brown and Stokely Carmichael," Hilliard continued. "Huey and the Black Panther Party are becoming known nationwide. Every day people call headquarters wanting to give money, start chapters. The second life of the Party has begun."

HAPPY BIRTHDAY HUEY

Fund Raising Birthday Benefit for

HUEY P. NEWTON

BY THE NEWTON-CLEAVER DEFENSE COMMITTEE

Sunday, Feb. 16, Berkeley Community Theatre

BERKELEY HIGH-SCHOOL AT GROVE & ALLSTON WAY **7:00 PM**

Speakers:
KATHLEEN CLEAVER
TOM HAYDEN
ATTORNEY CHARLES GARRY
FATHER EARL NEIL
RAY "MAASI" HEWETT LA BPP

WITH:
LE BALLET AFRO-HAITI
Rev. George Johnson & guitar
films: "Off the Pigs" &
"Prelude to Revolution"
Baby Dee reading the poetry of
Alprentice "Bunchy" Carter
Johnny Talbot & De Thangs

Indeed, the money flowed in from all over the place as the Panthers sponsored forums, workshops, and rallies on campuses, at churches and community organizations. Contributions came in from concerned individuals and support groups, including forerunners of the White Panthers, Grey Panthers, and the Young Lords. There was even a delegation calling themselves Honkies for Huey. If Newton was to have the proper representation during the upcoming trial, then buckets of donations were needed, the Panthers preached.

A decisive coalition was formed between the Panthers and the Peace and Freedom Party—a mostly white independent political party—and from this alliance additional money was raised in order to secure the services of attorney Charles Garry. Still another alliance was forged between the Panthers and leaders of the Student Nonviolent Coordinating Committee (SNCC). More than $10,000 was raised at a rally in Oakland that January featuring Carmichael, James Forman, and H. Rap Brown. The money lasted longer than the alliance.

While the Panthers intensified their fund raising activities, the "pigs" were turning up the heat. Not a day passed that didn't find a Panther caught in the cross-hairs of the police. The police harassed party members at every opportunity; early morning raids on the homes of the leaders were common occurrences; and there were rumors afloat that a massive attack on the Panthers was on the drawing board of the Oakland police (*see illustration on following page*).

Despite the constant raids and assaults, the Panthers continued to marshall support for their cause, although by April, 1968, there would be a double dose of tragedy.

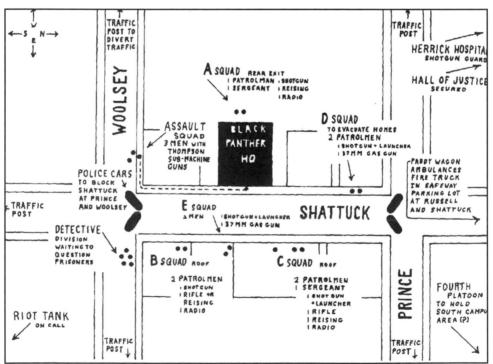

This map was drawn up by the Berkeley police in preparation for an August 30, 1969 raid on Black Panther headquarters.

The assassination of Dr. Martin Luther King, Jr. was a terrible blow for the entire nation, and the Panthers were not immune to the loss. Two days later, death moved closer to the Panthers.

According to one account, Eldridge Cleaver was leading a convoy of cars filled with Panthers bound for David Hilliard's house when he stopped the car to relieve himself on a dark street. "While I was in the middle of this call of nature, a car came around the corner from the direction that we ourselves had come, and I found myself in danger of being embarrassed, I thought, by a passing car," Cleaver remembered. "So I cut off the flow...and awkwardly hurried around to the other side of the car, to the sidewalk, to finish what had already been started.... But this car instead of passing, stopped, and a spotlight from it turned on and beamed my way. I could see it was the cops, two of them. They got out of the car and stood there....One of them shouted, 'Hey, you, walk out into the middle of the street with your hands up, quick!'"

"Hey, you, walk out into the middle of the street with your hands up, quick!"

37

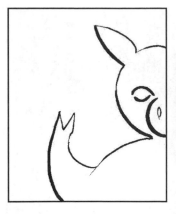  

Cleaver zipped up his pants and started for the front of his car. Suddenly, gunfire raked the night. Panthers took cover or scattered to nearby houses. Cleaver and Hutton scampered into the basement of a house. For over a half hour the shootout raged. Unable to roust them, the police hurled tear-gas canisters into the basement. One of them hit Cleaver in the chest. He had already been wounded in the foot by a ricocheting bullet. Suddenly the house was on fire, and Bobby and Eldridge had no choice but to surrender. After tossing their weapons out, Hutton and Cleaver came out of the basement. Cleaver was stark naked with his hands thrust in the air.

  The cops told both of them to hit the ground and spread-eagle. Once they were down, the cops dragged them to the squad cars. Cleaver said the next thing he knew, the cops were cursing and hitting them. "The pigs pointed to a squad car parked in the middle of the street," Cleaver said, "and told us to run for it. I told them I couldn't run.

"Then they snatched Little Bobby away from me and shoved him forward, telling him to run for the car. It was a sickening sight. Little Bobby, coughing and choking on the night air that was burning his lungs as my own were burning from the tear gas, stumbled forward as best he could, and after he traveled about ten yards the pigs cut loose on him with their guns."

39

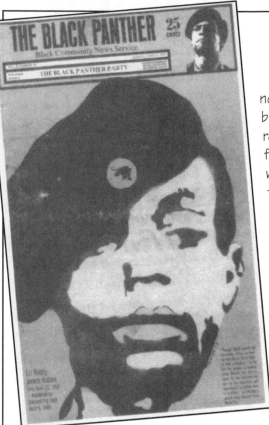

THE BLACK PANTHER 25 CENTS

Black Community News Service

THE BLACK PANTHER PARTY

Lil Bobby James Hutton

Little Bobby Hutton was not the Panthers' first martyr, but he was certainly the most revered. He was the Party's first real recruit, and now he was first of the key members to fall. Cleaver, having violated his parole, was taken to state prison. Later he was charged with three counts of attempted murder of policemen and three counts of assault with a deadly weapon. His bail was set at $50,000. But through a loophole in the law, Cleaver was released two months later.

The Panthers' Minister of Information was free, but its Minister of Defense, Huey Newton, was still locked up awaiting trial. It was time now for the courts to pass judgment on a man who led a group J. Edgar Hoover, director of the FBI, called ...

"...the greatest threat to internal security in the country."

Chief among the institutions that bolster capitalism, the Panthers often cited, was the criminal justice or "injustice" system. And now their leader was caught squarely in the web of it, facing a long prison term or execution if found guilty of killing Officer John Frey. In his quest to ensure a fair trial for Newton, Charles Garry's first strategy was to either quash the indictments brought by the grand jury or to disrupt the entire jury system. Both requests were denied. A trial date was set for July 15, 1968. The case read: **The People of the State of California v. Huey P. Newton.**

After several days and reams of testimony the jury was finally selected—none of them a "peer" of Newton's. The one Black man of the twelve was David Harper, and he was elected foreman. Newton's motive for killing Officer Frey and wounding Officer Heanes, the prosecution contended, was to elude arrest. Prosecutor Lowell Jensen charged that Newton was in possession of two matchboxes of marijuana and carrying a concealed weapon, which if discovered by the officers in Newton's car would have placed him in violation of probation. All of this was mere speculation since Newton was never officially indicted for these infractions.

41

"HUEY"

"HUEY"

"HUEY"

"HUEY"

"HUEY"

"HUEY"

"HUEY"

"HUEY"

"HUEY"

"HUEY"

Meanwhile, the Huey Newton Defense Committee gathered steam. They may not have raised all the money that was needed, but they did a good job of inciting the masses of young people who positioned themselves daily outside the Alameda County Courthouse—"Moby Dick" it was called by the demonstrators—where they kept up a noisy and boisterous vigil. "Roast the Pigs! Free Huey! Off the Pigs! Free Huey!" they screamed until they were hoarse.

At the end of the seventh week of a trial muddled with conflicting testimony and a divided jury, a verdict was reached. Newton was guilty of voluntary manslaughter and wounding Officer Heanes. Naturally, no one was satisfied with the outcome, least of all the Oakland police who on the night of the verdict drove by the Panther office and shot out the windows, ripping the posters of Newton and Li'l Bobby Hutton to shreds. With their leader on his way to four years in prison, the rest of the Panthers knew it was time to cool it for a while and find a new location for their headquarters. Literally and figuratively they dug in on Shattuck Avenue, about midway between Berkeley and Oakland, but their escape tunnels beneath the house became flooded by backwater from the subway system.

4

We want decent housing, fit for shelter of human beings.

43

CO INTEL PRO

Things were also going to hell at the Panther chapter in Los Angeles. Minor differences between the Panthers and Maulana Ron Karenga's "US" (first dubbed "United Slaves" by the media, but ultimately, "US" was us, Black folks) were distorted or blown out of proportion by the slimy tricks of the FBI and its **COINTEL-PRO** (Counter Intelligence Program).

> **"Minor differences... were blown out of proportion by slimy tricks of the FBI..."**

To provoke violence between the two groups, FBI agents faked letters and made phone calls to make it appear the Panthers were plotting to kill members of US, and vice-versa. A sample of the way the FBI tried to get one group to actually murder members of the other group is seen in a memo dated **November 29, 1968:**

44

> "The Los Angeles Office is currently preparing an anonymous letter for Bureau approval which will be sent to the Los Angeles Black Panther Party (BPP) supposedly from a member of the US organization in which it will be stated that the youth group of the US organization is aware of the BPP 'contract' to kill Ron Karenga, leader of US, and they, US members, in retaliation, have made plans to ambush leaders of the BPP in Los Angeles."

The FBI also produced and distributed cartoons with each side appearing to insult and ridicule the other. On January 17, 1969 this diabolical scheme reached a deadly conclusion. Black Panther leaders Alprentice "Bunchy" Carter and John Huggins were murdered by US members George and Joseph Stiner, and Claude Hubert, in a classroom at UCLA's Campbell Hall. "Apparently at the FBI's behest, the Los Angeles Police Department (LAPD) followed up by conducting a massive raid— 75 to 100 SWAT equipped police participated— on the home of John Huggins' widow, Ericka, on the evening of his death, an action guaranteed to drastically raise the level of rage and frustration felt by the Panthers assembled here.

45

The police contended that the rousing of Ericka Huggins and other surviving LA-BPP leaders was intended to "avert further violence," a rationale which hardly explains why during the raid a cop placed a loaded gun to the head of the Huggins' six-month-old baby, Mai, laughed and said...

"You're next!"

(From The COINTELPRO Papers, by Ward Churchill and Jim Vander Wall.)

46

These same tactics—provoking one side against the other—were used over and over again in various parts of the country, especially where the Panthers were actively seeking to forge alliances with other radical groups. No doubt some of this subterfuge was at play during the later ideological split between Newton and Cleaver, who with his wife, Kathleen,

"No doubt some of this subterfuge was at play during the later ideological split between Newton and Cleaver..."

fled into exile to Cuba and then Algeria in November 1968. Cleaver was fearful that having violated his probation during the shootout that left Hutton dead he had a one-way ticket back to prison. He was given sixty days to turn himself in, but Cleaver chose to run. The ex-rapist and acclaimed author had not lost his survival instincts.

There was a widely circulated rumor to the effect that Cleaver might have been an informer or government agent; but, to date, nothing has surfaced to prove that Cleaver or "El Rage," as he was euphemistically called by his detractors, was an agent provocateur. Some contend that it made little difference if he was or not, since many of his political decisions proved detrimental to the Party's development.

47

In any case, the FBI or the local law enforcement agencies really didn't need Cleaver anyway. Hardly a chapter of Panthers were free of infiltrators. It was jokingly said that if there was a meeting of ten Panthers, four of them were agents or informers. The Panthers Party was a mass-based organization, so it was hard to screen every person who walked in off the streets and expressed an interest in "dying for the people."

From the accounts provided by Darthard Perry, code name "Othello," we can discern how an informer worked to destabilize the Panther Party. Not only does "Othello" take credit, along with Melvin "Cotton" Smith, for gathering information that led to the raids on Panther offices in Los Angeles in the winter of 1968, he also had strong opinions about the men who had murdered Bunchy Carter and John Huggins.

OTHELLO:

> "I recognized George Stiner, Joseph Stiner, and Claude Hubert from seeing them...on the fourteenth floor of the Federal Bureau of Investigation building on several occasions in the company of Brandon Cleary, the man I had seen drive them away from Campbell Hall."

"Othello" was convinced that the three murderers were working for the FBI.

Further confirmation of this suspicion is offered by Mike Thelwell in his Afterword to Gilbert Moore's **Rage**. "The two Stiners and Hubert were convicted. At their trial, they say nothing to implicate the Bureau," Thelwell writes. "Shortly after their incarceration, California penal authorities claim not to be able to protect them from Panther partisans in the prison population, which could well have been true....The three are transferred out of maximum security San Quentin to a minimum security prison camp from which they 'walk away'; they have never been seen since."

49

Most students of African-American history know Gene Roberts as a police officer who infiltrated Malcolm X's organization and became his body guard. But Roberts did not fade into the woodwork after failing to protect Malcolm. His next assignment was to penetrate the Panthers. It is amazing that his cover was still intact, and shortly after Roberts joined the Panthers the plan was hatched to bomb five department stores in Manhattan on Easter weekend in 1969. **"This was William King's idea,"** Roberts told a reporter. King was a childhood friend of Roberts, and the informer vouched for his old playmate from the Bronx, which helped King get into the Panthers. **"My job,"** Roberts continued, **"was to case the joints and find the best locations to place dynamite and other explosives. Bloomingdale's, Abercrombie & Fitch and Macy's were three of the stores I cased. Plus, I did reconnaissance on the Brooklyn Bridge subway station, checking out the transit telephone** center. **I managed to get inside where the switchboard is and they showed me around. I saw the whole operation...I had to laugh at how easy it was to get in. Later, King and I went over to the 42nd Police Precinct, and King showed me where we could plant some explosives behind it. We even climbed into the Bronx Botanical Gardens and examined it as a possible site for explosives. It didn't make any sense to me, but I went along with them."**

50

Roberts swore that all of these tactics, the planting of explosives—ridiculous though it seems—were taken from the movie "The Battle of Algiers." The purpose was to create havoc, terror, and harassment. Having completed the reconnaissance, the Panthers then set about preparing the explosives. Roberts recalled that they gathered up gas cans, charcoal and other items to use in making their own gunpowder. But before they could complete the task they were notified that Cleaver was coming to town. Things were put on hold.

"Every time somebody came in town I was the duty driver," Roberts related, "so when a party was given for Eldridge...I was the chauffeur. Well, after we arrived at the party, Dhoruba Richard Moore and Lumumba Shakur continued to criticize my passing so near the police station. Dhoruba said, 'Don't you know that's the station that we just bombed?' I told them I didn't know that. But later I learned that they were talking about the bombing in January in which Joan Bird and others were arrested."

51

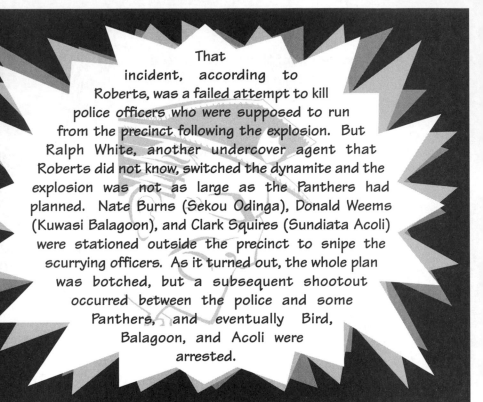

That incident, according to Roberts, was a failed attempt to kill police officers who were supposed to run from the precinct following the explosion. But Ralph White, another undercover agent that Roberts did not know, switched the dynamite and the explosion was not as large as the Panthers had planned. Nate Burns (Sekou Odinga), Donald Weems (Kuwasi Balagoon), and Clark Squires (Sundiata Acoli) were stationed outside the precinct to snipe the scurrying officers. As it turned out, the whole plan was botched, but a subsequent shootout occurred between the police and some Panthers, and eventually Bird, Balagoon, and Acoli were arrested.

Although Roberts was severely reprimanded for his driving blunder, his undercover role was not jeopardized. But he did have several close calls. On one occasion he was driving back to New York from Baltimore with four other well-armed Panthers. In the trunk of the car was a semi-automatic rifle they had picked up in Baltimore. They were on the New Jersey Turnpike when they heard police sirens. "When I pulled the car over to the side of the turnpike I was scared stiff," Roberts said. "I knew that if the Jersey trooper asked me to open the trunk all hell would break loose. Luckily, we only got a ticket for speeding and a reprimand."

He had another close call when he was wearing a wire. **"I didn't want to wear the wire but my supervisor insisted,"** Roberts explained. **"And, as fate would have it, the very day I'm wired up the Panthers decide to have a firing drill where targets are placed on one another's chests. King pinned the target on me** and he just missed detecting the wire. **It would have been all over for me if he had touched me in the wrong place."** A final narrow escape happened when Roberts was again chauffeuring a group of Panthers and they were stopped by a police patrol car. **"We were coming from downtown on Houston Street just before you get to the FDR Drive,"** Roberts said. **"There were five of us in the car—Dhoruba, King, Curtis Powell, and Mike Tabor—we were all armed. One of the officers approached the car and asked for my license and registration.**

53

"I explained to him that this was a rental car and I gave him the contract. All of the Panthers pulled their guns out. The officer stepped back from the car to read the contract. His partner was still in the patrol car filling out some papers or something. They were sitting ducks. The officer came back to the car and returned my papers and told me that I had a defective light in the back and that I should take care of it. I breathed a sigh of relief. I had no idea what I would have done if a shootout had occurred."

On April 2, 1969— exactly two years after Denzil Dowell was murdered by the police in Richmond, California— the possibility of further close calls for Roberts came to an end. Through reports and wiretaps, 21 Panthers were arrested and charged with arson, conspiracy, and attempted murder. Roberts was arrested along with the others, but following a sham booking process he was released. For the next several months Roberts lived in Virginia with his wife and daughter, a family the Panthers knew nothing about. In fact, the Panthers never knew where he

lived, where he worked or anything. "I knew everything about them, but they knew nothing about me," Roberts chuckled.

However, there were a few things that Roberts didn't know. He was unaware that there were other undercover policemen who had infiltrated the Panthers. Not until 1970, when the trial for the Panther 21 got underway, did the undercover officers come face to face with each other.

"There were six of us," Roberts recalled. "Ralph White, Carl Ashwood, Ray Fulton, Leslie Eggeslston, and Carl Wallace -- they all came out when I did."

None of them knew each other, and Roberts believed that this may have been deliberately done by the Bureau of Special Services to keep tabs on the informers, to check an informant's reports against another informant.

"There is certainly the possibility that undercover officers were reporting on undercover officers. I know I turned in reports in which I disclosed information about Ralph and others."

At the trial the Panthers were stunned to discover that Roberts was an undercover cop. Many of them shook their heads in disbelief. The reports submitted by Roberts and the others were only a dress rehearsal for their testimony during the trial. Of all those who testified for the prosecution, Roberts time on the witness stand was the least effective. Murray Kempton described Roberts perfectly in **The Briar Patch**, his book on the trial:

55

"Roberts withdrew further into himself and took to swaying back to await the question and forward to give the answer in the slow rocking of one who nods.... Nothing would provoke him; and it could be understood that, long before he came here, his private mind had measured out for him just how far he would go to damage these defendants and that now, having reached that stopping point, nothing, not even annoyance by hostile lawyers, would push him further."

During his time on the witness stand Roberts was inexpressive and beyond reserved, clearly trying to come to grips with his own guilt while working to ensure a guilty verdict.

"Get him away...he's the electronic nigger!" cried Dhoruba Moore when Roberts stepped down from the stand after completing his testimony. For the most part, the other undercover cops did no better. The prosecution could sense that its case against the Panthers was slipping away.

When it came time for the Panthers to speak their last words of the trial, Afeni Shakur was chosen. Shakur, whose son, Tupac, has had his own unfortunate day in court, went back over the record of the trial before warming to her closing argument. "I don't know," she said, "but I would appreciate it if you would end this nightmare, because I'm tired of it and I can't justify it in my mind. There's no logical reason for us to have gone through the last two years as we have, to be threatened with imprisonment because somebody somewhere is watching and waiting to justify being a spy."

57

"So do what you have to do," she pleaded, "but please don't forget what you saw and heard in this courtroom....Let history record you as a jury that would not kneel to outrageous bidding of the state. Show us that we were not wrong in assuming that you would judge us fairly. And remember that that's all we're asking of you. All we ask of you is that you judge us fairly. Please judge us according to the way that you want to be judged." Later, she would tell her friends that fear had pushed her to this level of eloquence.

It took the jury less than a half hour to find the defendants not guilty of all 156 counts. Even Dhoruba Moore and Mike Tabor, both of whom jumped bail with Tabor fleeing the country, were also acquitted. Thus, instead of being on a bus to Attica, the Panthers had been exonerated, although within a few weeks Moore would once more be in the clutches of his sworn enemies. That trial and its outcome would not be so kind—Moore would spend 19 years behind bars before winning his release in 1990.

5

We want education for our people that exposes the true nature of the decadent American society. We want education that teaches us our true history and our role in the present-day society.

By the time the Panther 21 were freed of all charges, the Party's Free Breakfast for School Children Program, first launched at St. Augustine's Church in Oakland, was more than two years old. From its inception it was seen as but one of several survival programs to be initiated by the Panthers. It began with the idea of collecting food and supplies from local merchants, David Hilliard explained in his autobiography. These hot meals were offered at St. Augustine's Episcopal Church under the auspices of a Party friend, Father Earl Neil. "The program grows naturally from our new lives," Hilliard said, "...[the] free food baskets, the need now to feed our own kids, our desire to show the community we do something more than shoot it out with cops.

We call the program a 'survival' program—survival pending revolution—not something to replace revolution or challenge the power relations demanding radical action, but an activity that strengthens us for the coming fight...."

> "The program... show(ed) the community we do something more than shoot it out with cops."

60

Much has been made of the free breakfast program, that food and groceries were donated by merchants under duress. "Many took issue not with the idea of feeding free breakfasts to kids," writes Hugh Pearson in **The Shadow of the Panther**, "but with the idea of trusting the Panthers to feed free breakfasts to kids."

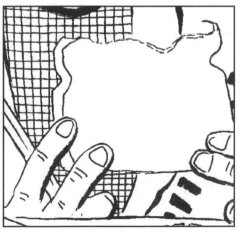

Nonetheless the program was highly effective, especially that phase of it conducted by college students in the Party. They "read up on price supports, discovering that dairy farmers dumped milk, butter, cheese and eggs, in order to guarantee a certain market price," Pearson discloses. "The party would send out ten to twelve Black Panthers to convenience stores, supermarkets, dairy suppliers, and restaurants to ask for donations. A restaurant making french fries everyday would donate bags full of potato skins it would otherwise throw away, which became the basis for the hash browns fed in the free breakfast program. A convenience store, such as the one in West Oakland, would donate a crate of eggs twice per month, while another would donate twenty pounds of bacon per month, and another twenty cartons of milk."

61

Assata Shakur, from her autobiography **Assata**, offers these pleasant memories about feeding hungry children: **"Working on the breakfast program turned out to be an absolute delight,"** she said. **"The work was so fulfilling. The Harlem branch had break-** fast programs in three different churches, and I rotated among all three. From the first day I saw those kids, my heart went out to them. They were such bright, open little people, each with his or her own personality. I spent the first two weeks or so just getting my cooking act together."

On the heels of this thriving innovation there was talk about the need for other survival programs, such as:

• A free medical clinic, where tests could be done for sickle-cell anemia;

• Free clothing and shoes;

• Free education and assistance for the elderly.

By 1970, the Panthers were involved in a number of pressing social issues. Panther Brenda Hyson led an assault against a state law which made legal abortions available to Black and poor women. From her perspective the "oppressive ruling class will use the law to kill off Blacks and other oppressed people before they are born." To her logic, voluntary abortion would lead to forced

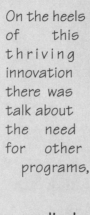

sterilization, and Black women had a political responsibility to oppose any form of "legalized murder." Though unconfirmed, there were reports that the Panthers were responsible for vandalizing Planned Parenthood Centers. Ironically, many of the programs established by the Panthers are currently under the jurisdiction of local, county, state and federal agencies.

Other social concerns were raised by the Panther women. Not for a moment did they believe the quote often attributed to Stokely Carmichael that the only position for women in the movement was "prone." Nor were they about to settle for some obsequious servant status. Their demand for equality and an end to abuse and forced rape did not come easily, but they kept up the pressure.

While there was no specific rule in the Panther bylaws that dealt directly with these problems, the leadership did occasionally address the issues.

"In the Black Panther Party," Bobby Seale proclaimed, "we understand that male chauvinism is directly related to the class society. In order to explain how the Party deals with male chauvinism, I want to point out how the Party thinks and how the Party understands things."

At great length, Seale then cited a few anecdotes of how beautiful women in the Panther Party deal with wolves, and in setting them straight entice the young men to join the Party.

"Personal relations now are based more on knowing people personally and humanly, on people coming and working together and functioning in the Party. Now when men and women meet each other, their relation comes out of common interests, common goals, to function in the Party as revolutionaries."

Elaine Brown

This idealistic aim, though, was often ignored, and sisters continually complained about aggressive males and their autocratic behavior. Not that the female Panthers harbored any illusion of the males living up to an imposed creed; they knew better.

"We knew brothers dragged their old habits into the Party," Elaine Brown explained in A *Taste of Power*, her absorbing memoir.

"The Party's role, however, was not limited to external revolution but incorporated the revolutionizing of its ranks. If, however, the very leadership of a male-dominated organization was bent on clinging to old habits about women, we had a problem. We would have to fight for the right to fight for freedom."

After all of his research, Hugh Pearson concluded that the male Panthers used an assortment of head tricks to have their way with the women of the Party. Pearson noted how one male member of the Panther leadership used his rank to gain favors and sex. "He and many other men in the Party would lay guilt trips on the women they desired, coercing them to bed, applying Marxist-Leninist ideology to the situation if the woman refused their advances:

'Here I am in the revolution putting my life on the line, and here you are denying me.'

The woman would be accused of harboring a petit bourgeois ideal-
ism that she needed to lose."

For the Panthers the police were the "pigs," but in the eyes of many
female Panthers there was no scarcity of male chauvinist pigs lim-
iting their growth within the Party. As usual, the men had a lot to
learn. Learning is a lot easier if you're alive. If you must
die, it had better be for a cause you believe in.

6

We want all Black men to be exempt from military service.

68

A fact that is often ignored about the Panthers is that there was a lot of love in the Party, love which figured prominently in the lives of such couples as the Cleavers, Bobby and Artie Seale, Ericka and John Huggins, David and Pat Hilliard, Geronimo and Sandra Pratt, Michael Tabor and Connie Matthews, and Fred Hampton and Deborah Johnson. But love among

revolutionaries has always been a matter of stolen moments, and a luxury that few could afford. This luxury of love was even more difficult for the Panthers as they struggled against a state power that was relentless in its determination to destroy them and the people they loved. There is no bloodier example than the brutal assassination of Fred Hampton by the Chicago police.

No Panther better personified J. Edgar Hoover's fear of a threat to internal security than Fred Hampton. Three years after the Party was founded it had mushroomed to more than 5,000 members (though some contend that the Party was never more than 2,000 at its peak) in chapters across the nation, and, because of Hampton's charisma and leadership, the Chicago branch was exemplary.

Formerly a youth leader in the NAACP, Hampton brought organizational skills and experience that few other Panthers possessed. On the surface, Hampton's floppy hats, sneakers, and sweatshirts might sucker you into believing that he wasn't all that formidable, when in fact he was highly principled, disciplined, quick thinking, and determined. His uncompromising integrity and zeal for the revolution made him even a larger threat, and when he began to negotiate an alliance with the dreaded Black Stone Rangers— a gang noted for its ruthlessness—the FBI and the Chicago police needed no further prompting. Hampton had to be removed.

To facilitate the murder of Hampton, someone had to infiltrate the Party, gain access to Hampton, and supply the cops with floorplans to his apartent.

William O'Neal was recruited and given the assignment. It did not take O'Neal long to weasel his way into the very core of the Chicago Panthers; in fact, much in the same manner as Gene Roberts had done in New York City, O'Neal became chief of security and Hampton's bodyguard. Under the instructions of his contact agent, O'Neal gave his masters the floorplan to Hampton's apartment and a list of the weapons stored there. O'Neal was with Hampton on the last night of his life, and allegedly spiked the Panther leader's Kool-Aid drink with secobarbital. With Hampton drugged, O'Neal's betrayal was complete; all that was left in the pre-dawn hours of December 4, 1969, was for State Attorney Edward Hanrahan to unleash his troops.

The police, armed to the teeth with sub-machine guns, semi-automatic rifles, and shotguns, burst into Hampton's apartment. Mark Clark (organizer of a Panther chapter in Peoria, Illinois and son of a prominent minister) and Brenda Harris were the first targets. Clark, 19, was shot point blank through the heart, and Harris was shot several times while she lay in bed. From O'Neal's floorplans, the police knew the exact location of Hampton's bed. **"Police in the front room sprayed the wall facing the bedrooms with machine gun fire,"** Curtis Black reported in the National Guardian. **"Many of the bullet trajectories converged at the head of Hampton's bed."**

Hampton's fiancée Deborah Johnson, then eight months pregnant, continues the story: **"I remember someone came and shook Fred and said 'Chairman, wake up, the pigs are coming....Then I saw flashes of light coming from opposite directions. Fred looked up real slow, he raised his head, then he lowered it and closed his eyes again. He never said a word."**

Ms. Johnson and others were then ushered into the kitchen by the police. Johnson recalled overhearing the police talking from the bedroom where Hampton lay mortally wounded. **"I heard someone say, 'He's barely alive, but he'll make it.' Then I heard a couple of shots, and a voice, 'He's good and dead now'."** The raid was over after 10 minutes of intense, continuous gunfire.

A federal investigation later determined that 90 bullets were fired by the police. At most, one was fired by the Panthers.

Two Panthers were killed. Four were wounded. One policeman was grazed by "friendly fire."

When the news of the raid spread, the Black community was outraged, and all the major civil rights organizations joined in a call for an investigation. The Panthers, with all of their branches under severe attack, were stunned by the execution of one of their top leaders. They were not surprised when a grand jury returned no indictments against Hanrahan or the police, despite finding that virtually all the gunfire was from the police. Hanrahan had cut a deal and the Panthers got the raw end of it. But that was just the beginning.

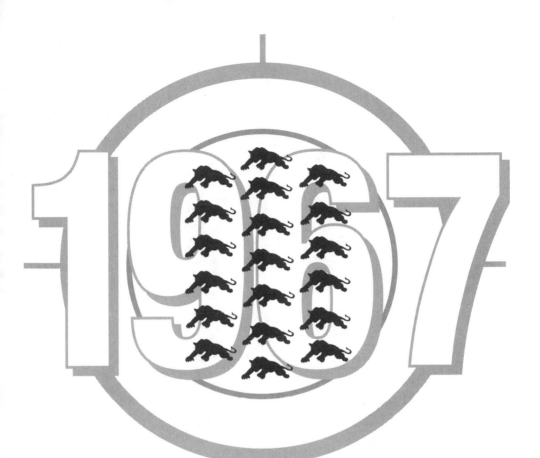

In the two-and-a-half-year period beginning in the spring of 1967, 19 Panthers were killed and more than a thousand were arrested. Police from one end of the country to the other bragged that 1969 was going to be the year of the dead Panthers; the hundreds of raids confirmed this objective. The raids came so fast that the Black Panther paper found it difficult to keep up with them. In 1969 alone, 27 Black Panthers were killed by the police; 749 were jailed or arrested. Before the Chicago assassination, there were concerted sweeps in Des Moines, Los Angeles, Indianapolis, San Diego, Philadelphia, and Detroit. The raid on the Detroit office was justified by the police as an attempt to find suspects in the Alex Rackley murder in New Haven, Connecticut. Rackley was accused of being an agent by George Sams, a fairly deranged person who had once been affiliated with the Student Nonviolent Coordinating Committee and had wormed his way into the Panthers. Sams moved furtively from one chapter to the next, under the guise of being a representative of the Central Committee.

73

After an intense interrogation, Sams and another Panther tortured Rackley, scalded him with hot water, and then killed him. According to the Panthers, Sams then dumped the corpse into a swamp and took off for parts unknown.

A nationwide search for Sams. was the pre- homes and offices of the Panthers. See- means of arresting key Panther leaders, inclu- Panther chapter, and Bobby Seale.

They were charged with two capital offenses: murder and conspiracy to commit murder. A six-month long trial ended in a hung jury in May 1971, after the judge dismissed the charges, claiming that there was no way the two of them would receive a fair trial, given the extensive media coverage. It was a second round of trials for Seale who had been arrested and tried on conspiracy charges stemming from the demonstrations in Chicago in August, 1968 at the Democratic National Convention. Because Charles Garry, who was the Panthers' lawyer, was

sick and unable to attend the proceedings, Seale sought to represent himself. His vigorous attempt to be his own lawyer was ultimately viewed by the judge as contempt of court. Seale protested the injustices and was eventually gagged, bound, and beaten. His case was arbitrarily severed from the other defendants, known as the Chicago Seven.

The government eventually dropped the charges against Seale for lack of sufficient evidence: however, the contempt charges remained.

text the police used to bust into the
king Rackley's killers would also be a useful
ding Ericka Huggins, head of the New Haven

For two years, Seale was kept in jail
without receiving a single conviction.

7

We want an immediate end to POLICE BRUTALITY and MURDER of Black people.

76

As if the Panthers, didn't have enough problems, they had to endure the siege from the squadrons of cops with two of their most dynamic leaders— Eldridge Cleaver and Huey Newton—either in exile or in prison. Facing charges of violating his parole for the shootout in which Bobby Hutton was killed, Cleaver let it be known to his comrades that he was not going to return to prison. His first option was to take a cache of arms, a platoon of Panthers and commandeer Merritt Junior College, turning it into a fortress in

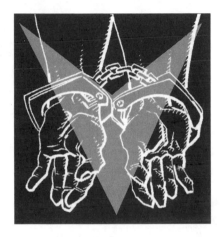

preparation for a gun battle with the authorities. When Newton heard of this, he quickly sent word from his prison cell to quash any such action. Cleaver, Newton decided, must leave the country for Cuba. Several plans were devised by the Panthers, but Cleaver had his own scheme for escape. "Escape was a very trying act," wrote Cleaver in **Soul on Ice**. "On the last afternoon in San Francisco prior to being hauled away to San

Quentin, Kathleen and I drove up to our house, pushed through the chanting demonstrators and stand-by police, and spoke a few words from the front porch. Then I went inside and there was Ralph Smith—a Panther who was a near double for me. In a moment, he and Kathleen returned to the front steps and continued the revolutionary rhetoric about not going to the pig prison.

77

"A couple of Panthers in the crowd were cued to ask 'me' questions which Ralph answered in grand style. Whites say that all niggers look alike, and Ralph and I fit the bill for the watchful authorities. As they continued this charade, I went out the rear door and over the back fence into a waiting car that took me to where I prepared for stage two of my goodbye to America.

"Rather carefully the M i m e T r o o p e r s made me up to look like a sick old man. They sliced some hair off my head and put on a mustache. They put me a baggy suit and shuffling shoes, and had me carrying an old briefcase under a black bowler hat. I wore thick glasses (which gave me an incredible headache) and did a lot of heavy breathing as we made our way into the San Francisco airport bound for JFK. Past security, past any questions or detention, this little old wheezing nigger was led by a young woman in

78

white who urged the flight crew to give me special

his cover was blown and the Cubans spirited him off to Algeria. The disenchantment with Cuba was mostly a result of the white Cubans locking up Black Panthers who hijacked planes and sought political asylum in the land of Castro.

atten-
tion on the trip
to New York. It was high drama, so effective that, en route, a stewardess, even gave me a shot of oxygen—my breathing sounded a little shaky to her."

Cleaver's Academy Award performance was enough to land him safely in Cuba where he remained for a year before

Things got off to a bumpy start for Cleaver in Algeria, but, thanks to the Vietnamese, Cleaver and the Panthers received international recognition and status.

In fact, the Vietnamese turned over their former residence on Embassy Row in Algiers to the Panthers, a location that provided them with public rooms, apartment, and a communication office complete with Telex equipment.

Based in Algiers the Panthers were in a position to take their struggle to a global arena. Cleaver and his entourage visited China, Korea, and North Vietnam. Asian goodwill, particularly the kindness and consideration extended by the Koreans and the Vietnamese, would sustain the

Asian goodwill, particularly the kindness and consideration extended by the Koreans and Vietnamese, would sustain the Panthers.

Panthers, whose relationship with the Algerians grew strained during that three-year period. Things had also worsened between Cleaver and Newton, as serious differences arose between them over the political and philosophical direction of the Party.

The problems between Newton and Cleaver had their origins in the murder of Fred Hampton. When Cleaver heard of the massacre in Chicago, he called for armed retaliation. Newton felt this was an adventuristic and dangerous option. The ideological split between Cleaver and Newton was all that COINTEL-PRO needed. Utilizing "disinformation," FBI agents fueled the split between the two Panther leaders. An FBI memorandum of May 1970 lays it out loud and clear:

"To create friction between Black Panther Party (BPP) leader Eldridge Cleaver in Algiers and BPP Headquarters, a spurious [fake, phony] letter concerning an internal dispute was sent Cleaver, who accepted it as genuine. As a result, the International Staff of the BPP was neutralized when Cleaver fired most of its members."

The fat was in the fire; the FBI turned up the heat by using a series of unsolved murders to create further dissension in the Panther ranks.

Having been freed in August, 1970 after serving three years in prison, Newton was now in position to deal directly with the issues tearing the Party apart. Beyond the disagreements with Cleaver, Newton was concerned about the condition of the Soledad Brothers— Fleeta Drumgo, John Cluchette, and George Jackson. They were nearing a trial for their lives on a trumped-up charge of murdering a prison guard. Newton was not back on the streets two days when another tragedy hit the Panthers: George Jackson's 16-year-old brother, Jonathan, impatient with the wheels of justice, took it upon himself to liberate the Soledad Three.

Newton was now in position to deal directly with the issues tearing the Party apart.

On August 7, 1970, Jonathan Jackson, with an arsenal of weapons under his coat, entered a courtroom in San Rafael, near the San Quentin Prison. **"We are the revolutionaries,"** Jackson cried to the startled people in the courtroom. **"All right, gentlemen, I'm taking over now!"** He freed three prisoners and took five hostages, including the assistant District Attorney and the judge, and then scurried across the Civic Center parking lot to a waiting van.

The nine people were not in the van five minutes before they were surrounded by the police, who opened fire. Jackson, the judge, and two of the prisoners were killed. His plan to hold the judge as ransom for his brother had tragically backfired. Newton delivered a moving eulogy at his funeral. A consequence of Jackson's bold action was the implication of Angela Davis, a radical intellectual and member of the Communist Party. Young Jackson had taken the guns in his possession from Ms. Davis's home, and though they were registered, a federal warrant was issued for her arrest.

With the Feds on her trail, Davis took flight and went underground. By the end of August, she was placed on the FBI's ten-most-wanted list, facing charges of murder, kidnapping, and conspiracy. Within two months she was apprehended in New York and extradited to California where she was incarcerated without bail. The Panthers, having expended lots of energy and funds to "Free Huey" now embarked on a "Free Angela" campaign, but they were just one among numerous organizations and individuals who worked for Davis' liberation. She was released on bail in 1972, and shortly thereafter acquitted of all charges.

8

We want freedom for all Black men held in federal, state, county, and city prisons and jails.

Meanwhile, the antagonism between Newton and Cleaver continued to roil. Cleaver, who had coined the phrase about being either part of the solution or part of the problem, had himself become a thorn in the side of the Party. Predictably, Cleaver and Newton disagreed over Jonathan Jackson's act. An action that was merely courageous and noble for

1968: BALLOT OR THE BULLET

Newton, in the eyes of Cleaver was the type of action the Panther Party should emulate. Jackson's devotion "has everything to do with the way the Black Panther Party was moving, helping to create the right climate, helping to discredit the judiciary and turn people against it so that the gun would be picked up," Cleaver said.

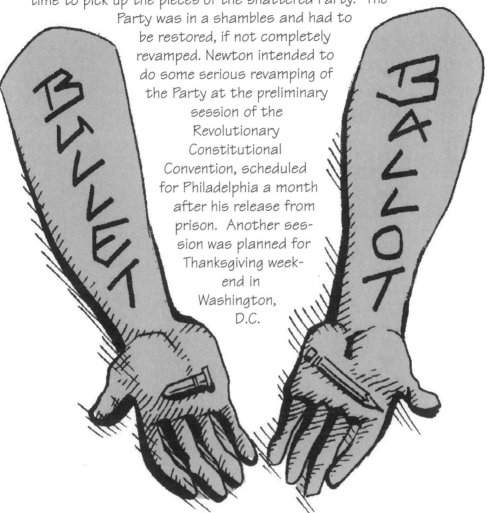

Newton disagreed: Instead of picking up the gun, it was time to pick up the pieces of the shattered Party. The Party was in a shambles and had to be restored, if not completely revamped. Newton intended to do some serious revamping of the Party at the preliminary session of the Revolutionary Constitutional Convention, scheduled for Philadelphia a month after his release from prison. Another session was planned for Thanksgiving weekend in Washington, D.C.

The purpose of the sessions, which had been largely devised by Cleaver while Newton was in prison, was to discuss the plight of Black people and to write a new Constitution of the United States. All of this struck Newton as a waste of time, since there was no way they could implement it. "I pushed the point of view that our most urgent commitment was to build a strong base of community support behind Bobby and Ericka, as well as the Soledad Brothers," Newton said in *Revolutionary Suicide*. "Eldridge expressed some agreement with me, and toward this goal we arranged for Kathleen Cleaver, who had great drawing power, to return and speak at the Washington session."

Newton himself would be the keynote speaker at the first session in Philadelphia, an event that was almost cancelled after the Panther headquarters in the "City of Brotherly Love" was raided by

the police. But the session had gathered national momentum, and there was no way the police were going to stop the convention. **"There were Indians, Asians, Puerto Ricans, White People, Black people,**

everybody," said Reggie Schell, then Defense Captain of the Panthers in Philadelphia. "Every ethnic group in the country was represented at that plenary session and any kind of clear cut, basic, fundamental plan to go back into

the communities ...could have helped us funnel more and more people into the struggle"

Sadly, Schell recalled, Newton's speech was a bust. "When he spoke to the people at that session, he spoke to ordi-

nary people in the street way over their head."

Newton was aware of his flop, but he blamed his failure more on his delivery than the content of the speech. "I am not a good public speaker, " Newton admitted. "I tend to lecture and teach in a rather dull fashion— but people were not responding

to my ideas, only to an image, and although I was very excited by all the energy and enthusiasm I saw there, I was also disturbed by the lack of serious analytical thought."

Huey was even more disturbed when he learned that Kathleen Cleaver was not coming to the session in Washington. Then he was told that Howard University, after promising to host the convention, had withdrawn its facilities. The Panthers were able to secure meeting places at several churches, but there was still a basic problem that could not be overcome: Many people had been attracted to the convention because of Cleaver's overblown rhetoric about overthrowing the government. That precipitated hundreds of letters from the more militant-minded Panthers, many of whom defected. To repair the situation, Newton began a national tour in which he visited Panther chapters all over the country. He was pleasantly surprised to discover how well-organized the Panthers were. Even so, Newton felt that they lacked the comprehensive ideology needed to analyze situations. That didn't sit well with many of the Panther chapters. They pointed out that it was not the lack of analysis that kept them reeling from one day to the next, it was the attacks by the damned police! Each city had its own special tale to tell about police atrocities.

Each city had its own special tale to tell about police atrocities.

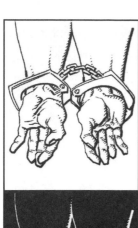

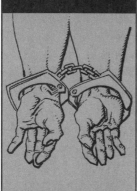

When the police felt disinclined to risk their own precious hides in gun battles, they fell back on "dirty tricks"; they devised a number of ways to frame the Panthers— especially the young, unsuspecting brothers.

What happened to David Rice should be a lesson to us all. Rice was a Panther leader in Omaha, Nebraska in 1970 when he was accused of first degree murder in the death of a police officer. Officer Larry Minard was killed by a booby-trapped suitcase in a vacant house. Later, when he heard the police were looking for him— they said they'd found dynamite in his house!— Rice turned himself in. In April 1971, based on the testimony of a youth who had been threatened with the electric chair if he didn't finger David Rice, Rice was sentenced to life imprisonment.

In Detroit, on Easter Sunday, 1971, Abdur-Rahman (Ron Irwin) led a group of Panthers on a raid of a suspected dope house. Their mission, Pat Fry of the *People's Daily World* related, was to confiscate and destroy the heroin ripping apart the community. "They planned to use the money they found for the Panthers' free breakfast program on the city's poverty-stricken east side," Fry reported.

"To their dismay, what they discovered was a communal home of 'hippies,' university students who, at most, may have had a few marijuana joints. While Abdur-Rahman

and another youth searched upstairs for drugs, the two other Panthers waited on the ground floor with a gun drawn on the students. As one of the students moved to quiet the dog, the dog jumped, and the gun accidentally went off, shooting the student who later died."

The Panthers were arrested and charged with first-degree murder; all of them except Abdur-Rahman copped pleas to lesser charges after agree-ing to give evidence against the others.

Only
later was it learned, after
Abdur-Rahman had been found guilty and
sentenced to life without parole, that the four
Panthers had been held in isolation and told they were
being prepared for a major drug bust.

"Evidence from police files released
under the Freedom of Information
Act points to one particular Panther
leader in Detroit as the agent who
directed the operation," said Fry.

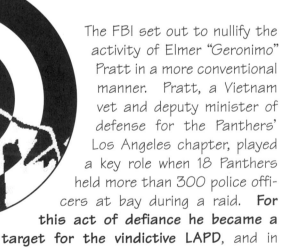

The FBI set out to nullify the
activity of Elmer "Geronimo"
Pratt in a more conventional
manner. Pratt, a Vietnam
vet and deputy minister of
defense for the Panthers'
Los Angeles chapter, played
a key role when 18 Panthers
held more than 300 police officers at bay during a raid. **For
this act of defiance he became a
target for the vindictive LAPD,** and in
1970, according to Daryl Grisby in his important but unheralded
book, **For the People,** they formed the "Pratt Task Force."

In 1970, Pratt was charged with a murder in Santa Monica. The key witness later proved to be an informant, and an FBI wiretap, which clearly showed that Pratt was in Oakland at the time of the murder, mysteriously disappeared. Pratt was convicted in 1972. He has been denied parole repeatedly and is currently the longest serving—and the most celebrated—political prisoner in the country.

With the Panthers in nationwide disarray, the tension between Newton and Cleaver reached a point of no return. The final rupture stemmed from Newton's relationship with Connie Matthews, who was his secretary after his release from prison. Matthews, who had joined the Party while living in Europe, had been sent to Oakland at the suggestion of Cleaver to work out of Central Headquarters. Resourceful and intelligent, Matthews took care of Newton's travel and speaking engagements, and otherwise coordinated his daily activities. There were times when Newton was less than satisfied with her work, but he kept her on at Cleaver's insistence.

In late 1970 Matthews married Michael "Cetawayo" Tabor, one of the Panther 21 and a dynamic speaker and organizer. He and Matthews suddenly disappeared one day, taking many of Newton's personal papers with them, the leader claimed. "Connie was not a citizen and would have trouble staying in the United States," Newton recounted in *Revolutionary Suicide*. "Cetawayo was a fugitive who could not travel easily outside the country unless he went to Cuba or Algiers." However, there was no time for Newton to dwell on their whereabouts; he had his hands full, getting ready for a major rally called the Intercommunal Day of Solidarity, scheduled for March 5, 1971.

Again, Kathleen Cleaver was slated to be the keynote speaker. While Newton made preparation for the event, he had a series of long distance conversations with Cleaver. Cleaver had some small reservations about strategy and tactics of the affair, but promised Newton that his wife would be there.

To promote the upcoming rally, Newton proposed that a TV appearance scheduled for him be arranged to include a telephone hook up with Cleaver from Algiers. Everything was fine until the call went through to Cleaver.

"At first I could not believe what he was doing. He launched into Party business—and not only into Party business but Central Committee business, beginning with the Central Committee's expulsion of Connie Matthews Tabor, Cetawayo Tabor, the New York 21, and Elmer "Geronimo" Pratt.... All these Black Panthers were guilty of serious offenses— actions that had jeopardized other comrades in the Party."

In his tirade, Cleaver did not attack Newton, but chose to denounce David Hilliard, blaming him for the Party's problems and ineffectiveness. Still, Newton was not ready to believe that Cleaver was trying to undermine the Party. After the show was over, Newton went to a pay telephone and called Cleaver back. He was not aware that Cleaver was

taping the call, tapes that would later be aired on NBC in New York. "It soon became clear that Eldridge had organized a plot to subvert the work of the Party," Newton realized. This outburst was followed by resignations from several key Panther leaders in New York and New Jersey. Cleaver's plan to disrupt the Party and undermine Newton's leadership was taking root. "The final evidence of the plot," Newton said, "came when Connie Matthews Tabor and Michael Cetawayo Tabor turned up in Algiers. Everything pointed to the fact that Eldridge had sent Connie here in October of 1970 with subversion in mind, and it finally came to pass in February, 1971. Eldridge's defection was now out in the open."

We want all Black people when brought to trial to be tried in a court by a jury of their peer group or people from their Black communities, as defined by the Constitution of the United States.

Gradually the Panthers turned on each other. Factions loyal to Newton set upon defectors who sided with Cleaver, and vice-versa. At long last the fratricide sought by the FBI through its COINTELPRO was taking place with alarming frequency.

First Robert Webb, a devout Cleaverite was shot and killed in Harlem. In apparent retaliation, Cleaver's minions abducted Samuel Napier, shot him six times and left his body to roast in a building they set ablaze. Newton's attempt at damage control focused mainly on the public appearances and empha- sizing the Panther's survival pro- grams—there were now thirty of them, including an ambulance service, a senior escort program, as well as dental and optometry programs. But none of these could remove the gangsterism that was increasingly prevalent. To ensure funding and support for its free breakfast program the Party launched a series of boy- cotts of local stores, which only further alienated the Panthers from the people they wished to serve.

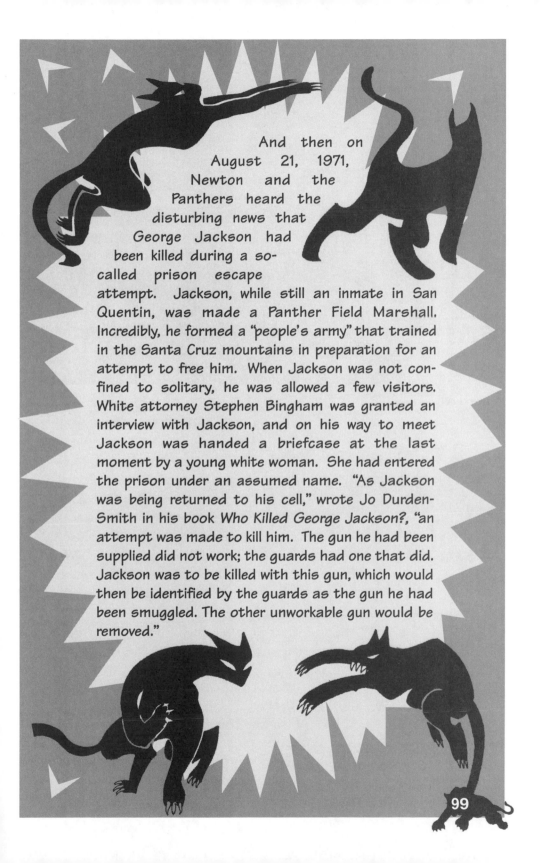

And then on August 21, 1971, Newton and the Panthers heard the disturbing news that George Jackson had been killed during a so-called prison escape attempt. Jackson, while still an inmate in San Quentin, was made a Panther Field Marshall. Incredibly, he formed a "people's army" that trained in the Santa Cruz mountains in preparation for an attempt to free him. When Jackson was not confined to solitary, he was allowed a few visitors. White attorney Stephen Bingham was granted an interview with Jackson, and on his way to meet Jackson was handed a briefcase at the last moment by a young white woman. She had entered the prison under an assumed name. "As Jackson was being returned to his cell," wrote Jo Durden-Smith in his book *Who Killed George Jackson?*, "an attempt was made to kill him. The gun he had been supplied did not work; the guards had one that did. Jackson was to be killed with this gun, which would then be identified by the guards as the gun he had been smuggled. The other unworkable gun would be removed."

However, their setup blew up in their faces when Jackson over-powered the guard with the gun and then proceeded to free other prisoners in the Adjustment Center. Two guards were killed immediately, then a third who arrived later. Realizing he and the others were doomed, Jackson chose to sacrifice his life, running out into the yard, where a bullet to the brain killed him instantly. One of the most daring of the caged Panthers was exterminated.

By 1972, the Panther mystique was fading; it was down to fewer than 200 core members, and the militant activism slowly dissipated, shifting more toward entrepreneurial schemes and electoral politics. "We were resurrecting Oakland & the World Entertainment, for the potentially lucrative business of concert promotion," Elaine Brown explained. "We would, Huey had assured the Central Committee as he outlined his new project, eventually become the sole concert promoters in Oakland." This venture never really got off the ground and floundered completely after an Ike and Tina Turner concert ended in a brawl. The assassination of an Oakland school superintendent, which was blamed on the Panthers, and the sensational exploits of Symbionese Liberation Army and its notorious leader, Donald "Cinque" DeFreeze, pushed the Panthers further into the background.

100

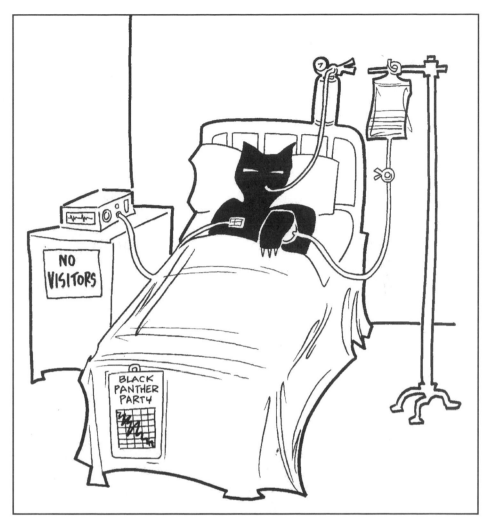

Bobby Seale's answer to the Party's dilemma was "internal improvement- ." And to this end, he became a drill sergeant, turning the Panthers into raw recruits as if they were in basic training. Where was Huey Newton during all

"(Bobby Seale) became a drill sergeant, turning the Panthers into raw recruits..."

this? Huey was relaxing in his penthouse overlooking Lake Merritt, occasionally scanning the horizon with his powerful telescope, and sometimes even looking directly into his old jail cell in the Alameda County Court-house.

BOBBY SEALE FOR MAYOR!

ELAINE BROWN FOR CITY COUNCIL

With Newton languishing in his apartment, snorting cocaine and fighting to remove a host of personal demons, Seale and Elaine Brown stepped up their political campaigns. Seale was running for mayor and Brown was seeking a city council seat. "When Bobby Seale landed a runoff spot for mayor of Oakland in 1973," Ken Kelley recorded in his memoir, "it marked the first time a black man had gone that far in Oakland politics. Although he eventually lost, his campaign changed the face of local politics forever—there may never be another white mayor in that city. The newly enfranchised black electorate began voting in black judges, black city councilmen, and black supervisors." Brown, too, was unsuccessful in her bid for office.

WHERE'S HUEY?

10

We want land, bread, housing, education, clothing, justice and peace. And as our major political objective, a United Nations-supervised plebiscite to be held throughout the Black colony in which only Black colonial subjects will be allowed to participate, for the purpose of determining the will of Black people as to their national destiny.

In 1974, there were a succession of startling developments that further shattered the Party. Newton and Seale who, except for imprisonment, had been inseparable, suddenly were at each others' throats. If Elaine Brown's account has any validity, a drug-ridden Newton literally whipped Seale out of the Party. Several minutes after a lively discussion about Seale's possible portrayal in a film, Newton got upset over a remark Seale made in reference to his cousin, who had bad-mouthed Newton. Newton was incensed

because Seale had not properly defended him during that encounter. "You're a punk, Bobby, and you can tell your m----- f---ing cousin I said that," Newton screamed. "You've been believing your own lies too long, Bobby, running around telling people you're the co-founder of the Black Panther Party...but you are not the co-founder...are you?!! Did you mention that to your cousin?" Newton continued to insult and humiliate Seale, Brown said, and Bobby was too terrified to respond. Then Newton ordered one of his bodyguards to get his bull-whip from the den.

"Bobby, you have violated the trust of the Party," Newton said. "...Take off your shirt and stand against the wall."

With Seale stripped of his shirt and facing the wall, Newton had his huge body-guard deliver twenty lashes to Seale's back. When the whipping was over, Newton told Seale that he was no longer chairman of the Party. "As a matter of fact, Bobby, I no longer want you in this Party." Seale was also told to vacate his residence and leave the city immediately. Two days later Elaine Brown assumed Seale's position as chairman of the Party. Seale seemed to have vanished into thin air until he surfaced a year later in Philadelphia. The expulsions continued. David and June Hilliard were next, then Bobby's brother, John. Newton's rage was not limited to Party members: He was arrested for shooting Kathleen Smith, a seventeen-year-old prostitute who had allegedly angered him by calling him "Baby Huey," a name he hated.

Kathleen Smith lingered in a coma for several months before dying.

105

A few days after Newton (allegedly) shot Kathleen Smith, he had a confrontation with his tailor, Preston Callins, and pistol-whipped him

so badly that the man required neurosurgery.

Out on bail for shooting Smith and beating Callins, Newton decided it was time to flee. "His lawyers and closest Hollywood friends got together

and had Newton and his principal companion, Gwen Fountaine (who became his wife), spirited through Mexico to the Caribbean coastline," Hugh Pearson reported. "From there they boarded a yacht. When they

reached the border of the international water limit and

the waters of Cuba, Huey and Gwen were placed in a rowboat to row the remainder of the way. But the boat capsized just before they made it. Huey could not swim. Gwen saved his life. They made it to the shoreline. The two were granted asylum by the Cuban government under the condition that Newton would keep his nose clean while living in Cuba."

It was a sorry state of affairs when Elaine Brown took over the Party. **"I watched them carefully,"** said Brown, recalling that Central

Committee meeting at which she took control. **"No one moved in response to my opening remarks. Here, I was a woman, proclaiming supreme power over the most militant organization in America. It felt natural to me. I had spent seven years as a dedicated member of the Black Panther Party, the last four at Huey's right hand."** And his lover, too, Brown should have added. An astute organizer, well aware of the Party's various financial holdings, Brown eagerly took the responsibility of stabilizing the Party. One of her first official acts was to hire a bookkeeper, Betty Van Patter, to handle the Party's complex business connections, including its umbrella organization, the Education Opportunities Corporation, and a night club owned by Newton's cousin, called the Lamp Post.

Van Patter's tenure with the Panthers was shortlived—she disappeared one night in December 1974 after complaining that the Panthers were misusing funds. Her badly decomposed body was later found floating in the Bay. She had been tortured and beaten to death.

Brown's second run for public office ended as the first one had—in defeat—but the exposure helped her land some choice civic positions. She was appointed to Oakland's Economic Development Council, and in 1976, she was one of Governor Jerry Brown's delegates at the Democratic National Convention. The Panthers had, by then, gone so legit that Brown was able to convince Mayor Lionel Wilson to join the Panther school board. After all, according to law enforcement agencies, the Black Panther Party was no longer the most feared group in America; that distinction now belonged to the American Indian Movement.

107

"The Party has become a political power in Oakland," David Hilliard announced when he was released from Vacaville prison. "Taking off its berets and leather jackets and putting on three-piece suits, the Party has realized Huey's vision of a 'people's political machine,' an organization that exercises influence at both local and state levels, forcing bureaucracies and institutions to address the needs of the black community, attracting accomplished intellectuals to aid in Party work, winning appointments and grants."

The changing political climate—Jimmy Carter in the White House, the Panthers growing more respectable by the day—presented a powerful allure for Newton, laboring as a carpenter in Cuba. He missed the limelight, and the daily phone chats with Brown only made him more homesick. Plus, Cleaver— having professed to have seen "Jesus in the moon"— had returned from exile in November 1975, to be quickly apprehended by the police; but by the summer of 1976, he had worked his way through a maze of legalities, raised the $100,000 bail, and was a free man. Soon, the man once thoroughly saturated in Marxist-Leninist ideology would be on his knees praying alongside Charles Colson, the born-again Christian who at one time had been a trusted aide to Richard Nixon.

Within a year Newton, too, was back in the states, receiving a hero's welcome at the Alameda Country Courthouse. Huey told the throng of well-wishers that, after three years in Cuba, he had come home to face the music.

The music consisted of one trial after another. Newton beat the Smith murder charges after the two trials ended in hung juries in 1979. His first trial for pistol-whipping Callins ended in a hung jury, and the second one ended in a mistrial when Callins refused to testify against Newton.

But into the 1980's, long after the dangerous Panthers had slinked off the scene, Newton was still hot copy for the media. To the media, Newton would continue to personify the Panthers, so, in his descent into crime and self-destruction, he disgraced not only himself, but the Black Panther Party as well.

In 1987, his fall from grace gathered momentum: He was convicted of being a felon in possession of a gun and served a year at the Jamestown Prison Camp; he was charged with embezzlement; in early 1988, he was jailed for six weeks for using drugs and driving under the influence in violation of his parole; in December 1988, he did six months in San Quentin for parole violation after being caught in a motel, free-basing cocaine with a prostitute.

Where were his friends when he needed them...after all he'd done for them?

Elaine Brown was somewhere in Europe trying to get her life back together. Cleaver was working the born-again Christian circuit (although he, too, would backslide and surrender to his hoodlum instincts before long).

109

Seale was daring to go where no man had gone before—seeking new ways to baste a slab of barbecue (see page 121). David Hilliard was negotiating his way through his own sea of demons... .

There was no girlfriend, no wife, no friends, no body-guards, no nothing on that August morning in 1989 when Tyrone Robinson put a bullet between Huey's eyes.

The streets that had spawned Newton, ultimately claimed him. But long before his physical death, Newton had released his will to live in bits and pieces and petty rages. It's unfortunate that his final days among crack addicts and petty thieves overshadow those furious nights and days when he defied the police who held his community hostage with its repression and brutality. But this is not the time for long laments or selective memories of what he stood for. We must take the whole man, all of him...all of him. He was neither Messiah nor Moses as some eulogies proclaimed; he was a young man created in an American ghetto who would not passively abide the limitations imposed by his overseers. The state and its lethal guardians- knew he was one of those "crazy niggers" that would never be still or pacified until he was dead.

Newton, like the rest of us, was imperfect, but we must grab what was most noble and admirable about his commitment and hold it up for emulation— the rest can be interred with his bones. He was symbolical of the Panthers mercurial flight, and what good traces he and they left behind can never be extinguished.

111

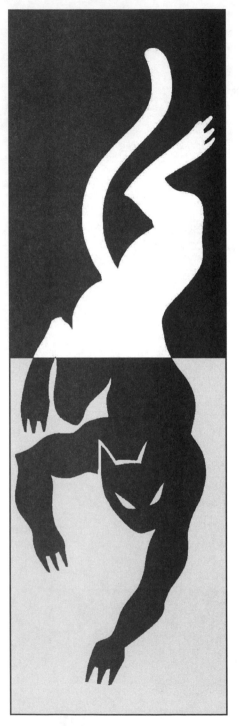

The Panther in his desperate boldness
Wears no disguise
Motivated by the truest
Of the oldest
Lies.

-- from **Black Panther**
Langston Hughes

The real legacy of the Panthers rests not with the Party's collection of bold leaders, but in the number of ordinary young people who grasp the spirit of their struggle, even if they never joined the organization.

To be sure, there were others who believed fully in the Party's militant commitment and saw armed revolt as the only alternative to ending oppression. Such was the aim of the Black Liberation Army, which, in many instances, was composed of former Panthers.

"According to the United States Senate Church Committee on terrorism in the United States," said Dhoruba bin Wahad (formerly Moore) in *Still Black, Still Strong*, **"the Black Liberation Army grew out of the Black Panther Party. The way it's portrayed in official documents is that the Black Liberation Army represented the hardcore militants within the BPP who were dissatisfied with legitimate struggle, with legitimate protests. Of course, that's not true. The racist repression of the Black Panther Party is what motivated the Black Liberation Army. The destruction of the Black Panther Party Into hostile factions, is what led to that particular development of the Black underground in the United States."**

113

Assata Shakur, no longer satisfied with the Panthers objectives and disgusted with Newton's expulsion of certain stalwarts, became a member of the newly formed underground, and she explained its structure:

"I was surprised to find that the Black Liberation Army was not a centralized, organized group with a common leadership and chain of command. Instead, there were various organizations and collectives working out of different cities, and in some of the larger cities there were often several groups working independently of each other. Many members of the various groups had been forced into hiding as a result of the extreme police repression that took place during the late sixties and early seventies. Some had serious cases, some had minor ones, and others, like me, were just wanted for 'questioning.' "

Shakur joined a cadre of other brothers and sisters who were totally committed to waging a revolution through armed struggle. They were all, as Shakur noted, interested in taking the struggle to a higher level, but were not exactly sure how to do it.

Several months later, Shakur lay in a hospital bed, close to death with her median nerve severed, handcuffed to her bed, as law enforcement officials hovered near, trying to interrogate her. Shakur had finally been apprehended by the police for her alleged role in several serious robberies by the Black Liberation Army (BLA), of which she was a member.

Above her picture in posters plastered in newspapers, subways, and post offices was a headline announcing a ten thousand dollars reward for information leading to her arrest and conviction.

"Everywhere I went," Shakur said in her memoir, "it seemed like I would turn around to find two detectives following behind me. I would look out my window and there, in the middle of Harlem, in front of my house, would be two white men sitting and reading the newspaper. I was scared to death to talk in my own house."

Having won acquittals in two previous trials, despite damning misinformation, Shakur was again facing charges after being arrested on the New Jersey Turnpike with fellow BLA members Sundiata Acoli and Zayd Malik Shakur, putatively the founder of the BLA. A state trooper and Zayd were killed in the shootout; Assata and another trooper were wounded.

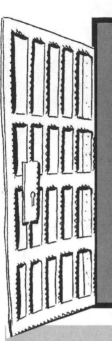

This time, though, she was convicted as an accomplice to the murder of a New Jersey state trooper and of atrocious assault on another. The state had manipulated facts and fabricated a tale to guarantee her conviction. Although even if she had participated in the shootout in the manner claimed by the prosecutors, her actions were armed self-defense and not "terrorism." She and Acoli were convicted for the death of the state trooper in separate trials. Both were sentenced to "Life plus thirty years consecutive."

Because of their political backgrounds, Shakur and Acoli were subjected to the harshest prison conditions imaginable. After six years of inhumane confinement, the BLA liberated Shakur from the Clinton Women's Prison in New Jersey. Later, Mutulu Shakur, not related to Assata, and white revolutionary Marilyn Buck were convicted of aiding Shakur in her escape. Buck was a former member of the Students for a Democratic Society, which was aligned with the white radical extremist group, the Weather Underground. Since her escape, Shakur has been living in Cuba.

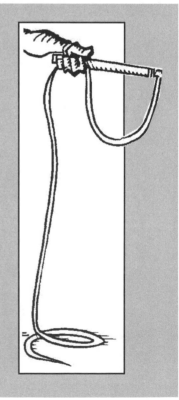

Those who were left in the Black Liberation Army, particularly after it allied with the Weather Underground in several ventures, were picked off one by one. Some members of the Black Liberation Army were also affiliated with the Republic of New Afrika (RNA). The RNA, whose primary objective was to carve out a "liberated zone" in the Mississippi River Delta, was also a target of CONINTELPRO.

As early as 1971 the FBI had provoked confrontations with the group and moved in to block its spread in Mississippi. In a resultant gun battle with the RNA, a police officer was killed and another wounded. Imari Obadele and 10 other RNA members were arrested and charged with murder, sedition, conspiracy, and possession of illegal weapons. They became the "RNA 11."

There have been several attempts to revive the Panthers, but the efforts have either petered out or are still in the embryonic stage. David Hilliard feels that it is fruitless to try to resurrect the Panthers. "Look, you can't reinvent the wheel," he told the press in 1993. "I was involved in the celebration to commemorate the 25th anniversary of the party and to put out a paper after Huey's death in 1989, and this was sufficient for me. You should understand that there are two Panther papers out there now, which is reflective of the continuing split by those who are interested in carrying on the Panther legacy and tradition."

117

One of the most promising efforts to restore the Panther tradition is with the folks connected to the newspaper Arm The Masses and December 12th Movement in New York City. The editorial of each issue of Arm The Masses proclaims:

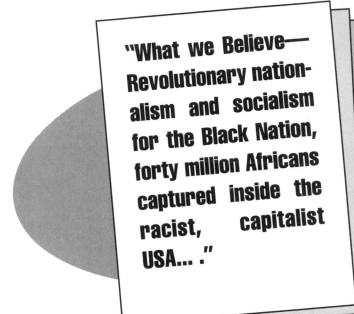

"What we Believe— Revolutionary nation- alism and socialism for the Black Nation, forty million Africans captured inside the racist, capitalist USA... ."

This powerful resolve is in keeping with the best of the ideals promoted by the Panthers.

So, too, is the commitment of CVGSheba Makeda Haven and the dedicated cadre of former Panthers who, since March 1991, have been struggling valiantly to put the Black Panther Paper in circulation. This paper should not be confused with The Commentator, says Haven. "That paper is the outgrowth of divergent points of view in the effort to sustain the legacy of the Panther Party," she explains.

"Our paper, as you can see from the listings that appear in the back of each edition, is focused on political prisoners and organizing to empower the community. There is currently no Black Panther Party, but we are trying to keep the spirit and commitment that they represented alive."

119

THE PANTHER PANTHEON

WHERE ARE THEY NOW?

BOBBY SEALE, the co-founder and chairman of the Black Panther Party, is currently busy promoting various projects, several of them directly linked to his Panther experience, including a feature film based on his life. He has authored two autobiographies, **Seize the Time** and **The Lonely Rage**, and a very popular cookbook, **Barbeque'n with Bobby**. Once a stand-up comedian and emcee, Seale made a cameo appearance in the film Malcolm X. As the creator-director of R.E.A.C.H., an organization dedicated to teaching community organizing, Seale travels and lectures widely. At Temple University, he is a voluntary community liaison and teaches in the school's Department of African and African-American Studies.

DAVID HILLIARD has been on tour recently promoting his highly acclaimed autobiography **This Side of Glory**. A lifelong friend of the late Huey Newton, Hilliard was the Party's chief of staff. He is a recovering addict who has been drug free for three years and is a representative for the United Public Employees' Union, Local 790, in Oakland. He lectures widely on his experience in the Party and continues to participate as a social activist for a number of vital issues.

ELAINE BROWN succeeded Bobby Seale as chair of the Party and held the position for three years. She now resides in France, where she is married to a French industrialist. Brown was unsuccessful in two bids for the Oakland City Council in 1973 and 1975. She recently authored a riveting memoir, **A Taste of Power**, which has been among the bestsellers at black bookstores.

ELDRIDGE CLEAVER continues to gather his share of notoriety and was most recently in the news after being charged with burglary. He still lives in California, but is no longer married to Kathleen, with whom he has two children. Following a conversion to Christianity— which he discusses in detail in his book *Soul on Fire*— Cleaver established his prison ministry, Eldridge Cleaver Crusades, and was for a while associated with the Mormons. There were rumors he was seeking to run again for office—he ran unsuccessfully for the U.S. Senate in 1986— on the Republican ticket but run-ins with the law may have torpedoed those plans.

KATHLEEN CLEAVER, after ending her marriage with Eldridge, received a law degree at Yale University and now is an instructor at Emory University Law School in Atlanta. A former Central Committee member of the Panthers, Cleaver is a dynamic speaker as well as a competent attorney. She retains a commitment to the Panthers, and this was exemplified with her recent attempt to represent longtime political prisoner, Elmer "Geronimo" Pratt.

ELMER "GERONIMO" PRATT is the longest serving political prisoner in the country. For 25 years Pratt has been behind bars at San Quentin, convicted of killing a woman in Santa Monica in 1968. Evidence, supplied by an informant, that he could not have been at the scene of the crime mysteriously disappeared. At the time of his arrest Pratt was the deputy minister of defense of the Party and head of the chapter in Southern California. In 1995, he was denied parole for the thirteenth time.

ERICKA HUGGINS was best known as the wife of her martyred husband, John, who was killed by members of US at Campbell Hall on the UCLA campus in January 1969. Moreover, the LAPD had the audacity to arrest Huggins and charge her with intent to commit murder. One of her chief tasks as a Panther was to direct the Oakland Community Learning Center, which she did with amazing results. It is rumored that she is working on her memoirs.

BOBBY RUSH, the congressman from Chicago, was deputy defense minister and head of the group's Chicago chapter. Rush was closely associated with the slain Fred Hampton, but left the Panthers shortly after Hampton's death. He was jailed in 1971 on a weapons conviction. In 1982, he was elected to the Chicago City Council. Rush has been relentless in his pursuit of restitution for the families related to Hampton and others killed in the 1969 raid by the Chicago police. He helped win the $1.5 million settlement from the city.

DHORUBA BIN WAHAD was freed from prison in 1990 after serving 19 years on a trumped-up charge. Wahad, then Moore, was a leader of the Panther chapter in New York City and one of the 21 arrested and tried for conspiracy. They were all acquitted, but Wahad was subsequently convicted of killing and wounding police officers in 1971. Since his release, he has been a tireless advocate on behalf of political prisoners and P.O.W.'s. A powerful and eloquent speaker as well as a prolific writer, Wahad has traveled extensively in Europe and Africa, including the Seventh Pan-African Conference convened in Uganda in 1994, where he was a delegate. He has recently established a base of operations in Accra, Ghana, with the aim of building an institution that will link the struggle of progressive Pan-Africanists and revolutionaries in the Diaspora with sympathetic governments in Africa. In this task, he is ably assisted by his wife and companion, Tanaquil. Wahad is also featured in a documentary, **"Passin' It On**," which recounts his early days as a Panther and his current advocacy of political prisoners.

EMORY DOUGLAS was the artist for the Black Panther paper which, at its peak, had a circulation of more than 130,000 copies per issue. His graphics depicting police officers as pigs were universally heralded. At present he is a graphic artist at the Sun Reporter in San Francisco.

124

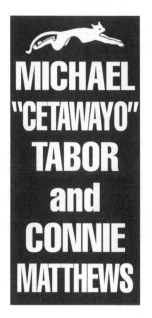

MICHAEL "CETAWAYO" TABOR and CONNIE MATTHEWS

MICHAEL "CETAWAYO" TABOR and CONNIE MATTHEWS are no longer a couple but for many years they were inseparable in their struggle for liberation as members of the Party. Matthews worked as Huey Newton's secretary, but eventually sided with the Cleaver faction, taking up residence in Algiers and later in Lusaka, Zambia. According to reports, she is now living in her native Jamaica. Cetawayo, who was one of the Panther 21, continues to live in Lusaka, where he is a highly respected communicator and activist. He has a radio show and directs a troupe of actors and dancers.

ASSATA SHAKUR

ASSATA SHAKUR was disenchanted with the Panther program and objectives, and after several key members of the Party were expelled in the early 1970s, she resigned. To express her committed political activism, Shakur next joined forces with a cadre of radicals—some of them former Panthers—who later became known as the Black Liberation Army. During one brutal encounter with the state police, Shakur was seriously wounded and later imprisoned. Charges against her were largely fabricated, but Shakur, with assistance from members of the Black Liberation Army, was eventually liberated from the Clinton women's Prison in New Jersey. She currently resides in Cuba with her daughter, and is the author of a compelling autobiography.

LANDON WILLIAMS has been often cited for his political integrity among the Panther leaders. Williams was the Party's security chief and helped to train members, since he was more educated than most Panthers. In 1978, he earned a master's degree in public policy from UC Berkeley and four years later was executive assistant to the chairman of Stanford University's Institute of Energy Studies. Today he heads an urban development program in Marin City, California and is an assistant manager for the city of Berkeley.

MUMIA ABU-JAMAL is an award-winning journalist, voice of the people, former Panther and political prisoner, who is on death row in Pennsylvania. Jamal was shot when he tried to stop a policeman from beating his brother. The policeman was subsequently shot by someone who witnesses claim ran from the scene. Jamal's commentaries that were prepared for airing on PBS and then cancelled have been published in a book titled **Live From Death Row**. His articles are syndicated in a number of Black weeklies and alternative papers around the nation.

Other lesser known Panthers who have made a mark for themselves include:

■ **PAUL COATES**, who is the president and founder of Black Classic Books in Baltimore;

■ **MICHAEL MCGEE**, a community activist and one-time alderman in Milwaukee, Wisconsin; and

■ **DONALD COX**, who for many years lived in Switzerland, but now resides in Brazil.

BLACK PANTHERS AND OTHER POLITICAL PRISONERS

127

SUPPORT THE CAPTURED WARRIORS!

Mutulu Shakur #83205-012
USP Florence-Ad. Max
5880 State Highway, 678
P.O. Box 8500
Florence, CO 81226

**Sundiata Acoli (Clark Squire)
#39794-066**
USP Allenwood, Unit 3
P.O. Box 3000
White Deer, PA 17887

Mondo Langa (David Rice)
P.O. Box 2500
Lincoln, NE 68520

**Abdul Haqq (Craig Randall)
#89T1710**
CCF Main, Box 2001
Dannemora, NY 12929-2001

Herman Bell #89-C-262
P.O. Box 338
Napanoch, NY 12458-0338

Gary Tyler #84156
Ash 4
Louisiana State Prison
Angola, LA 70712

**Jalil A. Muntaqin (A. Bottom)
#77A4283**
P.O. Box 140
Attica, NY 14011-0149

Ruchell Cinque MaGee #A92051
Pelican Bay CF
Crescent City, CA 95531

128

APPENDIX

Black Panther Party Program and Platform

What We Want, What We Believe (October 1966)

1. We want freedom. We want power to determine the destiny of our Black community.

We believe that Black people will not be free until we are able to determine our destiny.

2. We want full employment for our people.

We believe that the federal government is responsible and obligated to give every man employment or a guaranteed income. We believe that if the white American businessman will not give full employment, then the means of production should be taken from the businessman and placed in the community so that the people of the community can organize and employ all of its people and give a high standard of living.

3. We want an end to robbery by the CAPITALIST of our Black community.

We believe that this racist government has robbed us and now we are demanding the overdue debt of forty acres and a two mules. Forty acres and two mules were promised 100 years ago as restitution for slave labor and mass murder of Black people. We will accept payment in currency which will be distributed by our many communities. The Germans are now aiding the Jews in Israel for the genocide of the Jewish people. The Germans murdered six million Jews. The American racist has taken part in the slaughter of over fifty million Black people; therefore, we feel that this is a modest demand that we make.

4. We want decent housing, fit for shelter of human beings.

We believe that if the white landlords will not give decent housing to our Black community, then the housing and the land should be made into cooperatives so that our community, with government aid, can build and make decent housing for its people.

5. We want education for our people that exposes the true nature of this decadent American society. We want education that teaches us our true history and our role in the present-day society.

We believe in an educational system that will give to our people a knowledge of self. If a man does not have knowledge of himself and his position in society and the world, then he has little chance to relate to anything else.

6. We want all Black men to be exempt from military service.

We believe the Black people should not be forced to fight in the military service to defend a racist government that does not protect us. We will not fight and kill other people of color in the world who, like Black people, are being victimized by the white racist government of America. We will protect ourselves from the force and violence of the racist police and the racist military, by whatever means necessary.

7. We want an immediate end to POLICE BRUTALITY and MURDER of Black people.

We believe we can end police brutality in our community by organizing Black self-defense groups that are dedicated to defending our Black community from racist police oppression and brutality. The Second Amendment of the United States gives a right to bear arms. We therefore believe that all Black people should arm themselves for self-defense.

8. We want freedom for all Black men held in federal, state, county and city prisons and jails.

We believe that all people should be released from the many jails and prisons because they have not received a fair and impartial trial.

133

9. *We want all Black people when brought to trial to be tried in a court by a jury of their peer group or people from their Black communities, as defined by the Constitution of the United States.*

We believe that the courts should follow the United States Constitution so that Black people will receive fair trials. The 14th Amendment of the United States Constitution gives a man a right to be tried by his peer group. A peer is a person from a similar economic, social, religious, geographical, environmental, historical and racial background. To do this the court will be forced to select a jury from the black community from which the Black defendant came. We have been and are being tried by all white-juries that have no understanding of the "average reasoning man" of the Black community.

10. *We want land, bread, housing, education, clothing, justice and peace. And as our political objective, a United Nations-supervised plebiscite to be held throughout the Black colony in which only Black colonial subjects will be allowed to participate, for the purposes of determining the will of Black people as the their national destiny.*

IN CONGRESS, JULY 4, 1776.

The unanimous Declaration of the thirteen United States of America.

When in the course of human events it becomes necessary for one people to dissolve the political bands which have connected them with another, and to assume, among the powers of the earth, the separate and equal station to which the laws of nature and nature's God entitle them, a decent respect to the opinions of mankind requires that they should declare the causes which impel them to the separation.

We hold these truths to be self-evident, that all men are created equal; that they are endowed by their Creator with certain unalienable rights; that among these are life, liberty, and the pursuit of happiness. That, to secure these rights, governments are instituted among men, deriving their just powers from the consent of the governed; that, whenever any form of government becomes destructive of these ends, it is the right of the people to alter or to abolish it, and to institute a new government laying its foundation on such principles, and organizing its powers in such form, as to them shall seem most likely to effect their safety and happiness. Prudence, indeed, will dictate that governments long established should not be changed for light and transient causes; and, accordingly, all experience hath shown that mankind are more disposed to suffer, while evils are sufferable, than to right themselves by abolishing the forms to which they are accustomed. But, when a long train of abuses and usurpations, pursuing invariable the same object, evinces a design to reduce them under absolute despotism, it is their right, it is their duty, to throw off such government, and to provide new guards for their future security.

Black Panther Party --
MILESTONES

1966

- **October 15**: Huey P. Newton and Bobby Seale collaborate on a draft of the Black Panther Party 10-Point Program and Platform and found the Black Panther Party for Self-Defense.

1967

- **January 1**: BPP opens first official headquarters in a storefront on 56th and Grove Streets in Oakland, California, and began holding political education meetings.

- **February 21**: Two years after the assassination of Malcolm X, his widow, Betty Shabazz visits the San Francisco Bay area. The Panthers, providing security for Ms. Shabazz, are accosted by the police who insist of disarming them. Panthers cite their Constitutional rights to bear arms, and the police make no arrests. The incident is a source of favorable publicity for the Panthers.

- **April 27**: First issue of Black Panther, Black Community News Service, is published. The murder of Denzil Dowell by the police is the lead story. BPP organizes protests and garner more acclaim.

- **May 21**: BPP members show up at the State Capitol in Sacramento bearing arms. Bobby Seale reads "Executive Mandate #1," written by Newton and addressing the right to bear arms.

- **June 29**: Stokely Carmichael, former chair of the Student Non-Violent Coordinating Committee (SNCC), is drafted in the BPP and given the rank of Field Marshall.

- **October 28**: Huey Newton is returning home from a party celebrating the end of his parole when he and another Panther are stopped by the police. A shootout erupts and Officer John Frey is killed. Newton and another officer are wounded. No gun was found on Newton, who was later arrested and charged with murder, assault, and attempted murder.

- **February 17-18**: Two large "Free Huey" rallies feature James Forman, H. Rap Brown, and Stokely Carmichael as speakers. Each is given a position in the Party to help seal an alliance between the BPP and SNCC.

- **March 4**: FBI secret memos direct Bureau offices to "prevent the coalition of militant Black nationalist groups" and "to prevent the rise of a Black 'Messiah' who would unify and electrify the Black nationalist community."

- **April 4**: Dr. Martin Luther King, Jr. is assassinated, and the BPP pleas for calm in Oakland. While there are no major disturbances, many people appear at Panther headquarters requesting guns.

• **April 6**: Li'l Bobby Hutton, the BPP's first recruit, is slain by the police following a shootout. Eldridge Cleaver is wounded, arrested and jailed for parole violation. Other Panthers at the incident are charged with attempted murder.

• **July 15**: Huey Newton's trial begins at Alameda County Courthouse. Hundreds of people ring the courthouse and the event

receives worldwide attention.

• **September 28**: Huey Newton is sentenced to 2-15 years in prison. Police officers, incensed by the outcome of the trial, shoot out the windows of Panther headquarters and nearby apartment buildings. No charges are brought against them by Police Chief Darryl Gates.

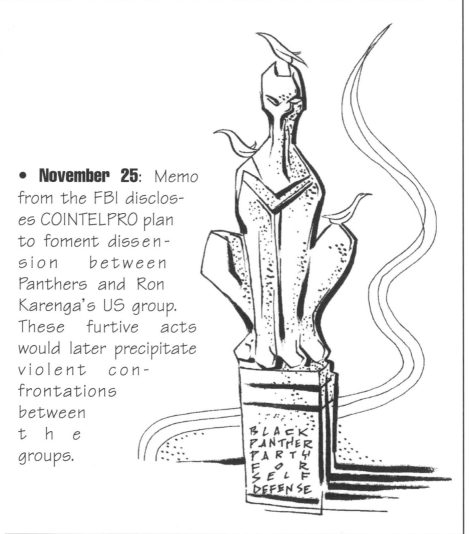

- **November 25**: Memo from the FBI discloses COINTELPRO plan to foment dissension between Panthers and Ron Karenga's US group. These furtive acts would later precipitate violent confrontations between the groups.

BLACK PANTHER PARTY FOR SELF DEFENSE

1969

- **January 17**: Alprentice "Bunchy" Carter and John Huggins, leaders of the BPP/Southern California chapter are gunned down on the UCLA campus by members of US. These murders coincided with raids on several BPP offices in the Los Angeles area.

• **April 2**: Twenty-one Panthers in New York City are arrested for allegedly conspiring to bomb local department stores. They are held on $100,000 bail.

• **July 18-21**: Panthers sponsor a highly successful United Front Against Fascism Conference in Oakland. A number of organizations, including the Young Lords, Young Patriots, Students for a Democratic Society, Republic of New Afrika, SNCC, and the Red Guard participate.

• **December 4**: Charismatic Panther leader Fred Hampton and Mark Clark are murdered in Chicago by the police. Hampton was noted for his dynamic speaking ability and organizing skills in the Chicago area. Most troubling the police was an alliance he was developing between the Panthers and the city's notorious gangs.

141

- **January 9**: Boston branch of BPP starts free clothing program.

- **April**: Panthers receive international support; solidarity committees from France, Denmark, Britain, Belgium, Netherlands, West Germany and Sweden convene in Frankfurt.

- **May 1**: A massive rally is staged on the New Haven Green to gather support for Lonnie McLucas, Bobby Seale and Ericka Huggins, all of whom are facing trial.

- **July 25**: Panther office in Omaha, Nebraska, closes after being bombed.

- **August 5**: After three years in prison, Huey Newton wins an appeal and is released.

• **August 7**: Seeking to liberate his brother George, Jonathan Jackson, 16, apprehends a judge and other hostages in a daring raid on a courtroom in Marin County. He provides weapons for Ruchell Magee, William Christmas and James McClain, who at the time are on trial. They make their escape in a van, but are fired upon immediately by the police. Jackson, McClain, Christmas and the judge are killed in the gun battle.

• **September 3**: BPP opens international section in Algeria under the aegis of Eldridge Cleaver.

• **November 7**: Southern California chapter Free Breakfast program serves over 1,700 meals per week; BPP/Boston program serves over 700 meals in a three-week period.

• **December 4-5**: Panthers convene Revolutionary People's Constitutional Convention in Washington, D.C.

143

- **January 16**: Panthers establish a legal assistance program in Toledo, Ohio, with 24-hour hotline and free lawyer services. Chicago Panthers provide door-to-door checkups and preventive health care information.

- **April**: Panther militants forced "underground," leading to the subsequent emergence of the Black Liberation Army.

- **April 10**: BPP initiates nationwide campaign to research and eradicate Sickle Cell Anemia, a deadly hereditary disease that afflicts Black Americans.

- **May**: Panther 21 trial ends after 26 months; all are acquitted, including Michael "Cetawayo" Tabor, Dhoruba Moore, and Edward Joseph Jamal in absentia.

- **July 23**: Former Panther, Michael "Cotton" Smith, testifying for the prosecution, admits he is long-time undercover agent during the trial of the LA 18.

- **August 21**: George Jackson, a BPP Field Marshall, is assassinated at San Quentin Prison during a so-called escape attempt. Jackson is shot down while running across the prison yard.

1972

- **February**: Huey Newton's first book, *To Die For the People*, is published to wide acclaim.

1973

- **March**: Newton publishes his autobiography, *Revolutionary Suicide*.

145

- **Summer**: Newton goes into exile in Cuba to avoid prosecution for the beating death of female barroom customer. Elaine Brown takes over as chair of the BPP.

- **Fall:** Eldridge and Kathleen Cleaver return from exile. Eldridge is a born-again Christian and four years later publishes **Soul on Fire,** which chronicles his religious conversion.

1988

• In separate incidents, Cleaver and Newton are arrested for drug possession.

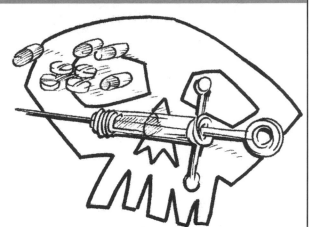

1989

• **August 22**: Newton is killed in a drug dispute on the streets of Oakland, not far from the site where he and Seale founded the BPP. Tyrone Robinson, member of the Black Guerrilla Family, is arrested for the killing.

1993

• A *Taste of Power* by Elaine Brown and **This Side of Glory** by David Hilliard are published. The books provide overlapping, and often contrasting, views of the inner workings of the BPP.

BIBLIOGRAPHY

Black, Curtis, "The Murder of Fred Hampton," in *The National Guardian News Weekly*, December 1989.

Brown, Elaine, **A Taste of Power**, Pantheon, New York, 1993.

Churchill, Ward and Jim Vander Wall, **The Cointelpro Papers**, South End Press, Boston, 1990.

Cleaver, Eldridge, **Soul on Ice**, Dell Publishing, New York, 1968.

_____ , **Soul on Fire**, Word Books, Waco, Texas, 1978.

Cluster, Dick, (Ed.), **They Should Have Served That Cup of Coffee**, South End Press, Boston, 1979.

Davis, Angela, **If They Come in the Morning**, New American Library, New York, 1971.

Durden-Smith, Jo, **Who Killed George Jackson?,** Knopf, New York, 1976.

Fletcher, Jim, Tanaquil Jones, and Sylvere Lotringer (Eds.), **Still Black, Still Strong**, Semiotext(E), New York, 1993.

Grigsby, Daryl Russell, **For the People**, Asante Publications, San Diego, 1987.

Hilliard, David with Lewis Cole, **This Side of Glory**, Little Brown, New York,1993.

Kelley, Ken, "Black Panther, White Lies," *California* magazine, San Francisco, August, 1990.

Kempton, Murray, **The Briar Patch**, E.P. Dutton, New York, 1973. Marable, Manning, **Race, Reform and Rebellion**, University Press of Mississippi, Jackson, 1984.

Moore, Gilbert, **Rage**, Harper & Row, 1971; Carroll & Graf, New York, 1993.

Newton, Huey, **Revolutionary Suicide**, Harcourt Brace Jovanovich, New York, 1973; Writers and Readers, New York, 1995.

Newton, Huey, **To Die for the People**, Random House, New York, 1972; Writers and Readers, New York, 1995.

Pearson, Hugh, **Shadow of the Panther**, Addison-Wesley, New York, 1994.

Seale, Bobby, **Seize the Time**, Random House, New York, 1970; Black Classic Press, Baltimore, 1991.

_____ ,**A Lonely Rage**, Times Books, New York, 1978.

Van Deburg, William, **New Day in Babylon**, University of Chicago Press, Chicago, 1992.

INDEX

150

HERB BOYD is an award-winning author and journalist who has taught Black Studies at the college level for nearly thirty years. He is the co-editor of **Brotherman: The Odyssey of Black Men in America -- An Anthology**, which was the recipient of the American Book Award in 1995. His history book, **Down the Glory Road**, has been widely acclaimed; his first publication for Writers and Readers was **African History for Beginners**. Boyd is a prolific journalist whose articles, essays and reviews can be found in more than a dozen publications, including Black Scholar, Black Enterprise, The Crisis, Class, the Amsterdam News, Detroit Metro Times, and the City Sun. He is currently an instructor of African American History at the College of New Rochelle in Manhattan and the New York City Technical College in Brooklyn.

LANCE TOOKS is a New York-based writer and illustrator. His love for arts can be traced to his family who encouraged him. Formerly, he worked as an assistant editor at Marvel Comics; did time as an animator for nearly one hundred commercials, films and music videos; created comics for Shade and Vibe magazines; drew four album covers for Pow Wow records; and illustrated a black inventors board game. His work includes **Divided by Infinity,** a self-published book**, Danger Funnies**, co-published with Cray for Dawn Press, and "Floaters," a five-issue miniseries edited by Spike Lee for Dark Horse comics. His comic strip, "Baby Ranks." which appears in the children's newspaper, Zuzu. is being developed into a children's book.

153

THE FOR BEGINNERS® SERIES

AFRICAN HISTORY FOR BEGINNERS:	ISBN 978-1-934389-18-8
ANARCHISM FOR BEGINNERS:	ISBN 978-1-934389-32-4
ARABS & ISRAEL FOR BEGINNERS:	ISBN 978-1-934389-16-4
ART THEORY FOR BEGINNERS:	ISBN 978-1-934389-47-8
ASTRONOMY FOR BEGINNERS:	ISBN 978-1-934389-25-6
AYN RAND FOR BEGINNERS:	ISBN 978-1-934389-37-9
BARACK OBAMA FOR BEGINNERS, AN ESSENTIAL GUIDE:	ISBN 978-1-934389-44-7
BEN FRANKLIN FOR BEGINNERS:	ISBN 978-1-934389-48-5
BLACK HISTORY FOR BEGINNERS:	ISBN 978-1-934389-19-5
THE BLACK HOLOCAUST FOR BEGINNERS:	ISBN 978-1-934389-03-4
BLACK WOMEN FOR BEGINNERS:	ISBN 978-1-934389-20-1
BUDDHA FOR BEGINNERS	ISBN 978-1-939994-33-2
BUKOWSKI FOR BEGINNERS	ISBN 978-1-939994-37-0
CHOMSKY FOR BEGINNERS:	ISBN 978-1-934389-17-1
DADA & SURREALISM FOR BEGINNERS:	ISBN 978-1-934389-00-3
DANTE FOR BEGINNERS:	ISBN 978-1-934389-67-6
DECONSTRUCTION FOR BEGINNERS:	ISBN 978-1-934389-26-3
DEMOCRACY FOR BEGINNERS:	ISBN 978-1-934389-36-2
DERRIDA FOR BEGINNERS:	ISBN 978-1-934389-11-9
EASTERN PHILOSOPHY FOR BEGINNERS:	ISBN 978-1-934389-07-2
EXISTENTIALISM FOR BEGINNERS:	ISBN 978-1-934389-21-8
FANON FOR BEGINNERS	ISBN 978-1-934389-87-4
FDR AND THE NEW DEAL FOR BEGINNERS:	ISBN 978-1-934389-50-8
FOUCAULT FOR BEGINNERS:	ISBN 978-1-934389-12-6
FRENCH REVOLUTIONS FOR BEGINNERS:	ISBN 978-1-934389-91-1
GENDER & SEXUALITY FOR BEGINNERS:	ISBN 978-1-934389-69-0
GLOBAL WARMING FOR BEGINNERS:	ISBN 978-1-934389-27-0
GREEK MYTHOLOGY FOR BEGINNERS:	ISBN 978-1-934389-83-6
HEIDEGGER FOR BEGINNERS:	ISBN 978-1-934389-13-3
THE HISTORY OF CLASSICAL MUSIC FOR BEGINNERS:	ISBN 978-1-939994-26-4
THE HISTORY OF OPERA FOR BEGINNERS:	ISBN 978-1-934389-79-9
ISLAM FOR BEGINNERS:	ISBN 978-1-934389-01-0
JANE AUSTEN FOR BEGINNERS:	ISBN 978-1-934389-61-4
JUNG FOR BEGINNERS:	ISBN 978-1-934389-76-8
KIERKEGAARD FOR BEGINNERS:	ISBN 978-1-934389-14-0
LACAN FOR BEGINNERS:	ISBN 978-1-934389-39-3
LINCOLN FOR BEGINNERS:	ISBN 978-1-934389-85-0
LINGUISTICS FOR BEGINNERS:	ISBN 978-1-934389-28-7
MALCOLM X FOR BEGINNERS:	ISBN 978-1-934389-04-1
MARX'S *DAS KAPITAL* FOR BEGINNERS:	ISBN 978-1-934389-59-1
MCLUHAN FOR BEGINNERS:	ISBN 978-1-934389-75-1
NIETZSCHE FOR BEGINNERS:	ISBN 978-1-934389-05-8
PAUL ROBESON FOR BEGINNERS	ISBN 978-1-934389-81-2
PHILOSOPHY FOR BEGINNERS:	ISBN 978-1-934389-02-7
PLATO FOR BEGINNERS:	ISBN 978-1-934389-08-9
POETRY FOR BEGINNERS:	ISBN 978-1-934389-46-1
POSTMODERNISM FOR BEGINNERS:	ISBN 978-1-934389-09-6
RELATIVITY & QUANTUM PHYSICS FOR BEGINNERS:	ISBN 978-1-934389-42-3
SARTRE FOR BEGINNERS:	ISBN 978-1-934389-15-7
SAUSSURE FOR BEGINNERS:	ISBN 978-1-939994-41-7
SHAKESPEARE FOR BEGINNERS:	ISBN 978-1-934389-29-4
STANISLAVSKI FOR BEGINNERS	ISBN 978-1-939994-35-6
STRUCTURALISM & POSTSTRUCTURALISM FOR BEGINNERS:	ISBN 978-1-934389-10-2
WOMEN'S HISTORY FOR BEGINNERS:	ISBN 978-1-934389-60-7
UNIONS FOR BEGINNERS:	ISBN 978-1-934389-77-5
U.S. CONSTITUTION FOR BEGINNERS:	ISBN 978-1-934389-62-1
ZEN FOR BEGINNERS:	ISBN 978-1-934389-06-5
ZINN FOR BEGINNERS:	ISBN 978-1-934389-40-9

www.forbeginnersbooks.com